BUILDING SMALL BOATS, SURF CRAFT AND CANOES IN FIBREGLASS

BUILDING SMALL BOATS, SURF CRAFT AND CANOES IN FIBREGLASS

(Materials, equipment, plugs and moulds, trouble shooting, repairs)

JOHN FLETT
JEFF TOGHILL

NAUTICAL

Published by Nautical Books
an imprint of
A & C Black (Publishers) Ltd
35 Bedford Row, London WC1R 4JH.

© Jeff Toghill 1981

Reprinted 1982, 1985, 1990

ISBN 0 7136 3283 6

A CIP catalogue record for this book is
available from the British Library.

Printed in Hong Kong through
Imago Productions (F.E.) Pte. Ltd.

CONTENTS

INTRODUCTION

GRP — glass reinforced plastic — is the simplest and most versatile of all materials used for the construction of boats and other water craft. Probably its greatest asset is that it brings quite complex boat building within reach of the average 'backyard' builder. Compared to other methods of construction, it requires relatively few skills and by following a few basic rules, even the most hamhanded amateur can make his own surfboard, canoe or fishing boat. There are no complicated drawings or plans to follow (unless you design and build your own plug first) and no careful measurements to set up. Once you have the mould, the process is — provided you are careful — both straightforward and simple.

Moulds can be purchased, hired, or taken off an original product. By following a few basic lay-up techniques, it is quite easy to run off one or more craft of quite professional standard. So easy, in fact, that often there is more work involved in the finishing of the product than in the making of it!

Just as simple is the procedure used for surfboards, skis and sailboards in which a GRP casing is placed around a preformed male mould or foam blank. The techniques of using the plastic material are similar albeit slightly different in application. The principal difference is that each surfboard uses a separate former or blank, while the female mould used for canoes, boats and yaks can be used over and over again.

This book is aimed at the 'backyard' amateur working in his tool shed or garage without the sophisticated refinements of a professional GRP factory. For this reason, technical details are kept as simple as possible without, of course, the loss of any accuracy or quality, and the techniques oriented to moulding with plastics in such an environment. There are no plans or measurements for each craft, only the quantities of materials required and the basic techniques for using them.

John Flett has taught fibreglass moulding professionally for many years. His technical information is reduced to a level that can be understood by non-technical readers. Jeff Toghill is a boating writer who has an intimate knowledge of boats built from the plastic material. Between them, they have translated a fairly technical subject into one that can be easily read and followed by even inexperienced builders. Dealing first with the basic materials and tools, they progress through a description of lay-up techniques to detailed information on how to mould individual craft ranging from a sizable fishing boat to a standard surfboard.

AUTHORS' NOTES

1 'Fibreglass' is a term widely used in many parts of the world to describe glass reinforced plastics (GRP). In the United Kingdom, however, 'Fibreglass' is a registered trade name and GRP is generally referred to as 'glassfibre'.

2 Wherever possible, the imperial and metric dimensions are given *as they are found in common usage,* and are therefore not a direct mathematical conversion. For example, chopped strand mat obtainable in the standard imperial measurement of 1 oz/ft^2 would have no direct metric equivalent. The standard metric measurement for similar weight material is 330 gm/m^2. This is not a direct conversion, but each measurement is the standard specification used to manufacture what are in effect the same weights of mat.

Similarly, metric and imperial measurements are sometimes mixed together, as with the resin/catalyst measurements, where the common usage is to measure the resin in pounds and the catalyst in millilitres.

1 MATERIALS

PLASTICS

This book is concerned with the use of a group of plastics known as polyesters. On their own, polyesters are brittle and lack strength but when reinforced with glassfibres they form an immensely strong laminate suitable for use as a building material. Plastics are man-made or synthetic materials chemically created from organic substances such as oil and coal tar. They are more correctly called polymers.

Polymers

Polymers are a group, or classification, of chemicals which is formed by chemical chains made up of smaller units hooked or linked together. The polymer changes from a liquid to a solid (usable state) by a cross-linking of the molecules in the chains.

This reaction is called *polymerisation*. Polymers fall into two distinct categories: 1 Thermoplastics; 2 Thermo-setting plastics (or thermosets).

Thermoplastics　Thermoplastics are polymers which can be converted from a solid to a liquid state by heat and revert to a solid again on cooling. This process can be repeated a number of times and a physical change effected without any chemical change taking place. Some examples of thermoplastics are: Acrylic, polyethylene, polyvinyl chloride.

Thermosets (thermo-setting plastics)　Thermosets are polymers which undergo a chemical change when formed or reacted and so cannot be reformed after completion of the reaction.

Polyesters fall into this category.

Polyesters　This class of polymer known as polyesters forms two groups: 1 Saturated; 2 Unsaturated.

We are concerned only with the unsaturated polyesters.

Unsaturated polyesters   These are 'unsatisfied' or reactive owing to their chemical make-up. They are exothermic (i.e. they give off heat) while polymerising. They are also thermo-setting. The word 'resin' is used to describe the liquid polyester when it is ready for use.

Unsaturated polyester resin   This is basically the product of a chemical reaction between two acids and an alcohol, which is then dissolved in a reactive monomer. Many other chemicals may then be added to this mixture to give the resin a variety of properties suitable for specific industrial application. Fast cure, slow cure, fire-retardant, translucent, thixotropic and elastic properties are but a few.

Unsaturated polyesters have the important property of being able to be 'cured' from a liquid to a solid state at room temperature, simply by adding two chemicals — a catalyst and an accelerator. No additional external heat or pressure is needed to cause the resin to polymerise.

Resins which can be 'set' in this manner are called 'cold cure' resins and it was their introduction on a commercial basis in 1945 which gave birth to the glassfibre reinforced plastics (GRP) industry as we know it today.

RESINS

Of the vast array of unsaturated polyester resins on the market the amateur GRP moulder would normally be concerned with only a few.

General purpose resin (laminating resin)

The most frequently used resin for laying up by hand, this resin is cheapest to buy and is used to impregnate the glassfibre reinforcement during the lay-up. It has a thixotropic agent added (usually aerosil) so that it will not leach or drain from vertical surfaces during moulding, and impregnates the glassfibre readily, making for easy lay-up.

GP resin has a similar consistency to oil paint and is usually purchased pre-accelerated with cobalt naphthenate, which gives it a minimum 3 months shelf life at 21°C (70°F). The cobalt also imparts a pink or purple hue to the resin. If purchased raw or 'straight' — without accelerator — it has a greatly extended shelf life of years rather than months, and it is clear in appearance.

Gelcoat resin

Usually called thixotropic resin, this is the first coat of plastic to be placed on the mould surface. It is brushed, rolled or sprayed onto the prepared mould and fulfils the following functions:

1 Creates a tough, resilient surface on the outside of the finished moulding.
2 Prevents the glassfibre laminates from showing through on the surface of the moulding.
3 Resists weathering and wear.
4 Allows the use of colours in the moulding by means of pigmentation.
5 Eliminates the need for any further surface finish.

Gelcoat resin is sufficiently thixotropic to allow it to remain on a vertical mould surface without 'curtaining' or draining. The ideal gelcoat thickness is about 0.5 mm ($^3/_{16}$ in). This is a coverage of approximately 0.5 kg (1 lb) per square metre of mould surface. While this is a handy rule of thumb method of calculating the gelcoat quantity required, always remember that it is safer to apply more rather than less.

Marine grade resins (gelcoat and laminating)

These are higher quality resins which give greater resistance to chemical attack and weathering, particularly when immersed in salt water. The superior properties of these resins are achieved by replacing the orthophthalic acid ingredient of the resin mixture with isophthalic acid, which results in a different arrangement of the acid groups and consequently gives a more chemically resistant and stronger polyester. This group of resins is known as 'Iso's'.

The glycol (alcohol) content of the resin can also be changed to upgrade the general performance and quality. Marine grade gelcoats and laminating resins are manufactured using neopentyl glycol (NPG) as the alcohol component (instead of propylene glycol). These are often referred to as Iso/NPG gel or Iso/ortho laminating resins.

Surfboard resins

These are basically the same as marine grade resins but have been formulated to give such properties as resilience, clarity, ease of wet-out and ease of flow. Three types of polyester resins are used in the manufacture of surfboards:

1 A laminating resin which is pigmented or tinted and used to lay-up the glassfibre reinforcement on the polyurethane foam blank.
2 A filler coat which is clear and fills and seals the glass cloth. It is spread evenly over the laminate with a rubber squeegee.
3 A gelcoat, also clear, which forms the outer smooth protective surface of the board. It is applied very thinly with a brush on top of the filler coat.

Flow coat resins

These are applied to the rough laminate or inside surface of the moulding after cure to give a smooth, clean, wear-resistant finish.

GLASSFIBRE

Many materials can be used as reinforcement for polyester resin — hessian, corrugated paper, cotton cloth, nylon cloth and carbon fibres, to mention a few. But by far the most suitable material is glass in a fibre form.

Production of glassfibre

Glass marbles are heated to melting point and continuous filaments of glass are drawn from their surfaces. From these filaments, glass strands are produced by a combing process while the filament is still in a molten state. Between 60 and 120 strands are then used to produce continuous filament rovings which are very flexible and immensely strong. The tensile strength of a glass filament is in excess of 2800 MPa (400,000 p.s.i.). Continuous filament rovings are the basis of most marketable forms of glassfibre reinforcement used with polyester resin.

The most common forms of glassfibre reinforcement available are:

Straight rovings   Supplied in a continuous coil, rovings are used in the form of chopped strands which are blown directly onto the mould surface, along with the laminating resin. This is done mechanically with a lay-up gun. Rovings have great uni-directional strength and are used in such items as fishing rods or bows and arrows. In boat moulding they may be used to provide added stiffness and strength at specific points in the moulding.

Woven rovings   These are available in various thicknesses and are used as reinforcement layers, usually sandwiched between layers of chopped strand mat, or as a simple means of adding bulk glassfibres to increase the stiffness of the laminate.

Woven glass cloth   This is the strongest form of glassfibre reinforcement, because of the close weave and the relatively large quantity of glass used. The thinnest cloths with the closest weave give the greatest tensile strength. In GRP laminations, this type of cloth gives a resin/glass ratio of 1/1.

Glassfibre tissue   This material is very thin and has negligible structural strength. It does, however, perform two useful functions when included in a GRP moulding:

1 When laid over a gelcoat it provides some reinforcement — resistance to gelcoat 'crazing' — and also helps prevent 'print through' of the pattern of subsequent laminating layers of glassfibre reinforcement.

2 It can be used as a finishing surface over the laminate inside the moulding, thus covering the rough appearance of the lay-up.

Glassfibre tape   Strips of woven cloth are known as tapes. They may be of varying widths and with open or closed weave. They are used mainly to join GRP or timber seams, provide local reinforcement or effect simple repairs.

Chopped strand mat (CSM)   This is the most common form of glassfibre reinforcement. Here the continuous filament rovings are chopped into short lengths of approximately 50 mm (2 in) and arranged at random in layers to produce a mat of glassfibres. The layers are sprayed with a chemical binder as the thickness of the mat is built-up. The binder or 'sizing' holds the fibres together and is soluble in polyester resin thus allowing easy and complete 'wet-out' of the reinforcing rovings by resin when laminating or laying up the moulding.

Chopped strand mat is usually produced in three thicknesses — 330 gm/m^2 (1oz/ft^2), 445 gm/m^2 (1½ oz/ft^2), 600 gm/m^2 (2 oz/ft^2), and gives a resin/glass ratio of approximately 2½/1.

Types of glass
There are two types of glass used in the manufacture of glassfibre reinforcement materials:

1 Soda-lime-silica glass, as used in windows. This is known as A grade glass. It has a high alkali content.
2 High lime, boro-silicate glass. This is known as E grade glass and has a low alkali content.

A grade glass has very good resistance to acid conditions because of its high alkali content. E grade glass, on the other hand, has greater resistance to alkali and water attack. It also has a high electrical insulation factor.

Different types of glassfibre have different strengths as well as different textures. Here, chopped strand mat (CSM) is being used to overlay a skin moulded with woven cloth.

OTHER MOULDING MATERIALS

Cold cure resins are usually dissolved in styrene monomer and can be made to set from a liquid to a solid state simply by the addition of either a suitable catalyst plus external heat or a suitable catalyst plus a suitable accelerator.

The second method is the most popular for general use as it allows the resin to 'set' or 'cure' at room temperature. The catalyst and accelerator immediately react together on mixing, instigating a chemical chain reaction which spreads to the main ingredients in the resin. As the reaction escalates, heat is produced within the resin. This production of heat from within the material is known as 'exotherm' or 'exothermic reaction' and is the chemical reaction which is vital to the whole glassfibre reinforced plastics hand lay-up process.

Catalysts (hardeners)

The catalyst normally used with polyester resins in the GRP hand lay-up process is the compound known as MEKP — methyl ethyl ketone reacted with hydrogen peroxide and usually supplied as a 60 per cent concentrated solution.

All organic peroxides are extremely reactive and corrosive and readily support combustion. MEKP is no exception and it is not normally available in its pure state as it is too explosive. It will burn skin tissue and cause irreparable damage to the retina of the eye in a matter of seconds. MEKP will attack most metals and so should be stored only in polyethylene or glass containers. It will also react with water or moisture, the usual result being a deterioration in its performance as a catalyst.

Safety precautions are vitally important when using this

CATALYST QUANTITIES REQUIRED

(Metric measures)

°C room temp.	*Gelcoat*	*Laminating resin*	
	Ml of catalyst/½ kg approx. 10 min working time	*Ml catalyst/½ kg*	*Approx. working time in minutes*
10°	11	—	—
13°	10	—	—
15°	9	6	40
18°	8	6	40
21°	7	5½	35
24°	6	5	30
27°	5½	4½	25
29°	5	4	20
32°	4½	3	15
35°	4	3	12

(Imperial measures)*

°F room temp.	*Gelcoat*	*Laminating resin*	
	Ml of catalyst/lb approx. 10 min working time	*Ml catalyst/lb*	*Approx. working time in minutes*
50°	10	—	—
55°	9	—	—
60°	8	5½	40
65°	7	5½	40
70°	6	5	35
75°	5½	4½	30
80°	5	4	25
85°	4½	3½	20
90°	4	3	15
95°	3½	2½	12

**Note:* While resin is always weighed in pounds when using imperial measurement, it is common practice to measure the catalyst in millilitres or cubic centimetres rather than fluid ounces.

chemical. If it comes in contact with the skin it must be washed off immediately, and if an eye becomes contaminated, immediate thorough irrigation with water is essential. This should be followed by thorough bathing with a dilute bicarbonate solution and medical help sought as soon as possible.

Being rich in oxygen MEKP is a potential fire hazard. So the rule is — no smoking in the workshop! Any spillage should be mopped up immediately and the rag or paper used placed in water. Given favourable conditions, this volatile chemical is capable of spontaneous combustion.

Normally between ¾ per cent and 3 per cent catalyst is added to the resin. This is a weight ratio calculated by the resin manufacturer. Too much as well as too little catalyst can adversely affect the laminate. Too little catalyst can cause permanent undercure while too much will speed up the curing to the point where it may become unusable. Care must be taken when measuring catalyst and weighing resin quantities, and the use of accurate measuring equipment is essential if the best results are to be obtained.

Accelerators (promoters, activators)

Almost all cold cure resin systems require the use of an accelerator since MEKP does not produce a fast enough polymerisation of the resin by itself. A typical unaccelerated resin with 1 per cent MEKP for example, will set in two to eight hours depending on the room temperature. An accelerator, as the name suggests, speeds up this process by reacting with the MEKP and reduces the curing time to minutes.

The accelerators normally used in polyesters are cobalt salts and anilines. The cold cure polyester resins usually make use of cobalt naphthenate although sometimes dimethyl aniline is used along with cobalt if a rapid cure resin is required. Cobalt is blue in colour and so its use as an accelerator imparts a pinky or bluish tinge to the resin. Normally, polyester resins (both laminating and gelcoat) are supplied pre-accelerated by the manufacturer. Although this gives the resin a limited useful storage or 'shelf' life

(approximately three months at 21°C (70°F)), it is an important safety feature, since if the catalyst and accelerator come into direct contact while being added to the resin a violent reaction can result. For this reason, only pre-accelerated resins should be used for hand lay-up work.

Colouring agents

These fall into three categories: pigment pastes, pigment powders and dyes.

Pigment pastes   These are mainly mineral oxides, finely ground and dispersed in a type of polyester resin. Pigments must have a high degree of opacity, have good heat and light stability and be compatible with polyesters. A maximum of 10 per cent pigment paste, by weight, is added to gelcoat resin, depending on the colour density of the pigment.

If pigment is added to the laminating resin as a 'back up' to the gelcoat colour in lightweight mouldings, only 2-5 per cent need be used. As a general rule the minimum quantity of pigment which gives a satisfactory colour density should be used as all additives tend to adversely affect the mechanical, and in some cases the chemical, properties of polyesters.

Powders   These are similar in opacity to paste pigments but are much more difficult to mix into the resin. As the powder is stirred in, tiny air bubbles get caught in suspension in the resin, and these can spoil the gelcoat appearance and affect its durability. For this reason they are seldom used except in specialist work.

Dyes   Used in translucent GRP sheeting such as corrugated roof-lights, shower panels, lamp shades and various lightweight mouldings which have no gelcoat. Depending on the depth of tinting required, between 2 and 10 per cent of liquid dye is added to the resin.

Paint pigments and tintings should not be used in polyester resins as they are incompatible with the resin and will almost certainly be detrimental to its cure.

Fillers

There are many fillers which can be added to polyester resin so that specific properties can be achieved and particular jobs tackled.

It is essential that any polyester filler be:

1 Completely dry — even slight dampness of the filler can inhibit the resin cure.
2 Chemically inert — i.e. must not react with the resin.
3 Easily mixed into the resin — only finely ground powders or pastes which disperse smoothly and easily through the resin should be used.

Fillers, when added to polyester resin in the correct proportions, impart a variety of properties but there is one property common to all — they increase the viscosity of the resin. Thus the addition of cabosil or aerosil as a thixotropic agent produces gelcoat resins. These substances are extremely light in weight and so increase viscosity with a minimum increase in density.

Other common fillers are normally used to change the resin from a liquid to a paste or putty and have a wide variety of useful applications, such as car body repair work, GRP repair work, as a jointing compound for mouldings and as a stable filler compound within a GRP moulding.

Apart from inducing the correct degree of viscosity to the resin for particular applications, fillers can impart additional properties which include:

1 An increase in the compressive strength of the resin.
2 An improvement in colour density or opacity of the filled area.
3 A reduction in the contraction of the resin during cure thus reducing the risk of cracking within the filled area.
4 Ease of 'cutting back' in repair work.
5 As a cost reduction factor by making the expensive resin go further.

Other materials can also impart particular characteristics to the resin. To mention but a few: *Marble dust* and *metal flake* can give attractive reflective surface effects to a moulding or casting.

Asbestos and *antimony oxide* provide fire retardant properties when mixed with a GRP laminate.
Silica powder is an extremely hard substance and is used for abrasion resistance.
Graphite and *iron powder* can give specific electrical properties.

Mixing   The usual proportion of filler to resin ranges between 25 and 50 per cent depending on application. Fillers are generally thoroughly mixed into the resin before the catalyst is added although it is possible for the resin to be catalysed first, and the filler added afterwards. The disadvantage with the latter is that working time is ticking away as the filler is being mixed in. However, this is offset by the extra mixing which ensures that the catalyst is thoroughly dispersed throughout the resin — an important factor where damp filler or absorbent substances such as sawdust are used, as these can sometimes inhibit a complete catalytic action.

It is important to note two points with regard to filled resins. First, most fillers have a slightly inhibiting effect on the resin cure, thus pot life is usually fractionally increased. And second, always add catalyst in percentage proportion to the weight of *resin* used — not to the total weight of the mixture.

Mould release agents (parting agents)

Waxes   These are polished into the surface of the mould to prevent adhesion of the gelcoat. Mould release wax must be silicon free since silicon waxes polish by scratching a microscopic layer from the surface being treated. In the case of a GRP mould this would allow the gelcoat to bond to the mould with disastrous results. Any non-silicon wax polish is suitable but special preparations, based on carnauba wax, have been formulated for the GRP industry and these should be used in preference to bees-wax based furniture polishes.

Mould release wax must be applied carefully as a build-up of wax can cause sticking of the moulding which will spoil the mirror-smooth surface of the mould. The wax should be applied in a circular motion, preferably by hand, or in the case of a large mould, with a slow-revving, clean polishing mop. On a new mould at least 6 coats of wax should be applied, each being polished to a high shine after about 15-20 minutes drying time on the mould surface.

Polyvinyl alcohol solution (PVA) This substance consists of polyvinyl dissolved in water or surgical spirit. The solution is water soluble and so washes off the mould and moulding surfaces easily after use. The PVA solution normally has a dye added as a coverage indicator on coloured or white mould surfaces. If the mould surface is black, the dye will not show up but coverage can be checked by working towards a light source such as a window.

PVA forms an excellent 'back up' mould release agent when used on top of a surface treated with mould release wax. It should be applied in a thin film with a sponge rather than with a brush as streaks or moist areas may be left under the surface skin of the PVA as it dries, resulting in gelcoat problems. Spray-on mould release agents and emulsion waxes are also available and if used carefully will give good results. However, for amateur use the wax and PVA coats are best.

In professional work, the PVA release agent is often omitted once the mould has been 'broken in' — thoroughly waxed and used for a number of mouldings. This saves valuable time in mould preparation as the PVA film must be washed from the mould surface after each 'pull' and the mould rewaxed. Rewaxing is a hard, time consuming job so it is worth taking a little time and trouble to obtain a good surface on the mould which will then allow a number of mouldings to be 'pulled' before rewaxing. The secret lies with a *thorough* preparation of a *perfect* mould surface.

Flow coat (wax in styrene)

This is the name given to a solution of paraffin wax dissolved in styrene monomer. It is used as an air barrier or 'surfacing agent' in flow coat resins, casting resins and repair work. Its function is to exclude air from the surface of the resin and so allow complete polymerisation to take place. The presence of air inhibits total cure of polyester resin thus leaving the lay-up surface slightly 'tacky' or sticky. This is a desirable feature when laying up a moulding, as successive layers of reinforcement can be applied over a period of hours or even days, without losing good bonding properties, but it does not make for a good hard surface finish.

For this reason most gelcoat and laminating grades of resin contain only small quantities of wax, and some laminating resins can be purchased completely wax free (or air inhibited) for use in large mouldings. When the lay-up has been completed, and all jointing and bonding of fittings carried out, the sticky, fibrous inside surface must be given a brushing out, or flow coat, of laminating resin containing 2-5 per cent wax in styrene. The wax floats to the surface, forms an air barrier and allows total cure of the resin. Flow coats are normally pigmented and give the inside surface of the moulding a smooth, clean, weather and wear resistant finish.

Cellophane or polythene sheeting can also be used as surfacing agents. When pressed on to the surface of the laminate they form an effective air barrier but are tedious to apply and have to be removed once the cure is complete.

Solvents

There are two solvents suitable for cleaning polyester resin from hands, tools, clothing, etc. — ethyl acetate and acetone. Acetone is cheaper and more effective with uncured polyester resin so it is the normal choice. It is available in chemically pure, industrial and re-claimed grades, the latter two being quite adequate for normal GRP work.

Three points should be noted with regard to acetone:

1 Acetone is only effective in dissolving *liquid* resin. Once the resin has set the acetone becomes ineffective and cannot 'save' a brush or roller. You must get into the habit of cleaning all implements in acetone *immediately* after use or, in the case of a large lay-up, at regular intervals during the work.

2 Acetone should not be used as a thinner for polyester resin for although it will reduce the viscosity effectively, its addition to the resin could lead to problems such as pre-release in the gelcoat or undercure in the laminate. Brushes and rollers which have been cleaned in acetone should be washed and dried before re-use to avoid such problems.

3 Acetone is a highly flammable liquid with a lower flash point than petrol and so it should be used with care and treated with respect, at all times.

2 TOOLS AND EQUIPMENT

SETTING UP A GRP WORKSHOP

Hand lay-up of a moulding is a messy business. No matter how careful you are, the workshop will gradually become contaminated with resin, laminate off-cuts, and other bits and pieces, so it is essential to cover the floor and work surfaces with polythene sheeting or some similar material to prevent damage.

The GRP workshop can be a very simple shed or garage area. Provided the mould can be worked on easily and there is enough space to cut the glassfibre material and decant and mix the resin, any workshop will suffice.

For preference, however, the work area should incorporate the following features:

1 Isolation from other buildings, both for fire safety and to avoid complaints about the smell of the styrene gas given off during cure of the laminate.
2 Good lighting so that even tight corners of the work can be clearly observed.
3 A power outlet so that power tools, fans and heaters can be plugged in.
4 A sink with running water, preferably hot.
5 Good ventilation — a most important feature.
6 A roller mounting, with a cutting area beneath it, so that chopped strand mat, cloth or woven rovings can be easily rolled out and cut to the required shape and length.
7 A means of conveniently storing the basic tools and equipment required for the GRP technique, i.e. a wall mounted 'shadow board' for the tools, brushes and rollers and a shelf, cupboard or bench top for the pigments, polish, catalyst, etc.

Mounting the glassfibre roll over a work bench prevents distortion of the mat and makes for easy cutting.

The average garage makes an ideal workshop provided a few basic factors are observed and — of course — the family car is removed!

8 Ideally, a work area which can be controlled to provide a still, dry atmosphere at around 21°C (70°F) with no draughts or dusty conditions.

9 A large waste disposal bin.

Glassfibre, especially chopped strand mat, readily absorbs moisture from the air. This moisture prevents complete 'wet-out' of the fibres by the resin and also inhibits the total cure of polyester. For this reason, fibreglass materials should always be kept wrapped up in polythene when not in use. Avoid moulding in extremes of temperature — below 12°C (53°F) and above 30°C (86°F) — as problems can arise which could adversely affect the cure of the resin. High humidity can create the same problems, so climatic conditions at the time of moulding must be carefully assessed. Draughts passing over a mould can cause patchy setting of gelcoats and undercure of the laminate.

It is a wise procedure to avoid working in sunlight, especially through glass, as the temperature variation between a sunlit area and a shaded area of the workshop can be enormous. The pot life of the resin can be drastically reduced in such conditions, resulting in the resin being wasted or, much worse, setting on the job before the laminate is wetted out and the trapped air expelled. Another problem associated with sudden increase in mould temperature is the risk of styrene loss from the resin leading to permanent undercure.

TOOLS

These are few and simple and are mostly basic wood and metal working tools. Minimum requirements for an average sized GRP moulding would be:

Stanley knife, plane blade and 25 mm (1 in) chisel

These are used to trim the GRP laminate at the 'toffee' stage before the moulding cures completely.

Tinsnips

Occasionally used to trim laminate edges after cure.

Coping saw

Used to trim, shape and make cut-outs in the laminate after cure. The coping saw will cut very thick laminates neatly and efficiently although the blades must be replaced frequently as they blunt quickly. However, these blades are cheap and easily fitted and don't 'bind' while cutting, thus making the coping saw a useful cutting tool for GRP.

Power jig saw

The 'professional' method of cutting GRP is by using one of these power saws. However, if the work is to be done quickly and neatly, the right blades must be used. Wood cutting blades should be avoided as they become worn very quickly. Metal cutting blades are suitable and will last for a reasonable length of time, but give a very slow cut. The most effective blades for GRP are tungsten carbide edged blades. Although relatively expensive, they are well worth the investment as they cut cleanly and quickly.

Power drill
High speed steel drills and carbide tipped drills will bore out GRP laminate effortlessly and will keep their edge for much longer than carbon steel drills. Care must be taken to avoid chipping the gelcoat from the laminate when drilling from inside the moulding. Slow drill speeds and masking tape or a backing block of timber held behind the area to be drilled can overcome this problem.

Files
Bastard and single cut tooth patterns are most suitable. The woodwork rasp is too coarse and tends to tear the laminate and chip gelcoats. It also gets blunt very quickly. Surform files and planes are most efficient for GRP work and their blades can be replaced cheaply and easily. Round and half-round metalwork files are also useful.

Pop-riveter
This tool is very useful for securing metal fittings of all types to GRP. Washers should be placed over the rivet shank on the inside of the job in order to spread the load, and to prevent the rivet from pulling through the laminate when being squeezed.

Abrasive papers
80 grit garnet paper is useful for removing the sharp edges of a moulding and for smoothing down the inside surface prior to applying a brushing-out coat. 40 grit garnet paper is the best grade to smooth and shape a polyurethene foam surfboard blank prior to lamination.

Silicon carbide paper (wet and dry) is indispensable for cutting back plugs, moulds and mouldings. 240 grit wet and dry paper is used for initial cutting or for coarse work with 320 or 400 grit paper used to follow up, the work finally being cut back with 600 or 800 grit paper. Liquid abrasives can be used on the GRP surface for fine finishing, with Brasso as good as any. However, these liquids will only bring up a lustre on the mould surface if 600 or some finer grade of paper has been used previously.

Points to note
1 Using liquid abrasive compounds over the coarser grades of silicon carbide will only result in the scratches produced by the paper being accentuated and a poor mould surface resulting. Fine grade paper must be used before liquids.
2 Always use the abrasive paper wet. A little soap in the water will help wash the paper and make it last longer.
3 Always use the paper with forward and backward strokes parallel to the length of the mould as a circular action creates circular scratches and makes it more difficult to achieve a high lustre finish on the mould surface.

LAY-UP EQUIPMENT
Most of the basic tools required for hand lay-up of GRP fall under the headings of brushes and rollers.

Brushes
These should be of a size appropriate to the lay-up job. 120 mm (5 in) brushes are best for large mouldings such as canoes, dinghies and surf-skis, while 25 mm (1 in) and 50 mm (2 in) brushes are useful for small mouldings, repair work and securing small fittings to the laminate. Brushes should have genuine hair bristles (some plastic bristles are affected by acetone when cleaning) and an unpainted wood or plastic handle. A painted handle will be attacked by the acetone which will dissolve the paint and make a mess of the brush, which in turn may cause staining of the resin. Brushes are the basic tool for moulding GRP and are used to apply both gelcoat and laminating resin, therefore it is worthwhile obtaining good quality brushes so that they can be cleaned and re-used a number of times.

Lambswool, mohair, or sponge rubber rollers
These are used to apply resin to large areas of chopped strand mat

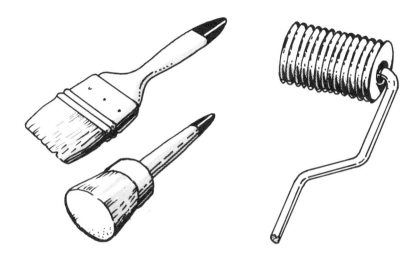

Broad brushes for laying on a good thickness of resin and 'stipple' brushes for working it through the glassfibre reinforcement are two of the most useful tools in GRP work. Vaned or washer rollers compact the laminate and squeeze out air bubbles — an important factor in the lay-up process.

The squeegee is used for a number of GRP jobs, but nowhere is it more important than when making a surfboard or sailboard.

or cloth quickly and efficiently. The roller does not replace the brush but is used in conjunction with it to roll and stipple the resin thoroughly through each fibre of the laminate.

Metal washer or vaned rollers

These are produced in a variety of lengths, diameters and materials such as steel, brass, aluminium tinplate or nylon. Their function is to compress the fibres of the laminate after thorough soaking with brush or roller and to squeeze out trapped air. The most efficient rollers are those with the thinnest washers, or vanes, as they compress the laminate without squeezing the resin from the fibres, and leaving thin 'resin starved' lines in the laminate.

These 'compression' rollers should be used on all but the smallest mouldings, as they increase the density of the laminate thus giving a much stronger job than that obtained by using brushes. They also enable more efficient use to be made of the laminating resin. As each layer of glassfibre is soaked with resin and then rolled down with the compression roller, excess resin is brought to the surface along with the expelled air. This resin then soaks into the next layer of mat.

The aim in laminating a mould is to 'wet-out' the glassfibre reinforcement material thoroughly, but with the *minimum* quantity of resin. Compression rollers are the best tools to use for this.

Rubber or plastic squeegee

The squeegee is used to spread a thick coat of resin quickly and evenly over a flat mould surface. Its use is usually restricted to fairly specialised work such as applying the filler coat of resin to the cured laminate when building a surfboard.

Measuring equipment

Since, as mentioned earlier, the mixing of chemicals must be done accurately if good results are to be achieved, then it is obviously important that accurate measuring equipment is used at all stages. The basic requirements for all but the largest mouldings are:

Scales   Resins are measured by weight rather than volume, so a simple but accurate set of kitchen scales should be placed securely at a convenient height to perform this task.

Graduated liquid dispenser   Some method of measuring accurately the catalyst is necessary before it can be mixed with the resin. It is more convenient to dispense the MEKP (methyl ethyl ketone peroxide) by means of a liquid measure rather than by weight, and almost any accurate graduated container can be used. But by far the safest and cleanest method is to use a sealed, graduated catalyst dispenser specially made for this job. These containers allow the catalyst to be measured and poured in one easy move without risk of spilling. Also, should the catalyst be knocked over the polyethelene bottle will not break and only the small quantity of fluid in the measuring tube will be spilled.

Thermometers

It is essential when moulding to determine the working temperature in the room, and keep track of any fluctuations. A couple of simple thermometers hung around the room will suffice — say one near the windows and one in the most shaded part of the workshop. Room temperature can greatly affect the 'pot life' or working time of the resin, and therefore it is important to be aware of any temperature fluctuations if the job is to be kept under strict control.

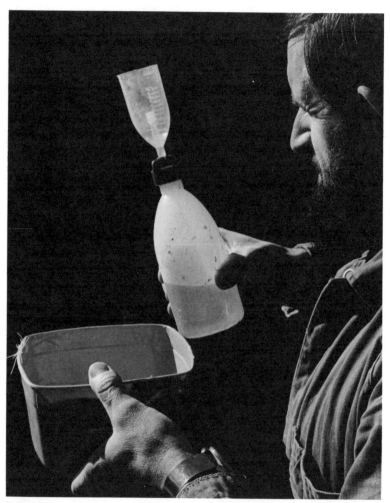

Specially made graduated liquid dispensers not only provide for very accurate measurement, but also reduce the risk of injury from large quantities of corrosive liquid being spilled if the bottle is knocked over.

ANCILLARY EQUIPMENT

When working with GRP many items other than the equipment mentioned should be kept at hand to avoid delay or frustration. These are mostly indicated by common sense and experience but a few of the more important ones are:

Containers

For mixing and applying the resin. Rimless tins (such as large size fruit and vegetable tins), PVC or polyethelene ice-cream containers are the most suitable and easily acquired. Beware, however, of the polystyrene ice-cream container and vending machine drinking cup as polystyrene is dissolved by the styrene in the resin. Waxed paper cups are also useful for mixing small quantities of gelcoat and laminating resin.

Polishing cloths and waxing rags

Cheesecloth is the most suitable material for polishing GRP moulds after application of the carnuba wax mould release. Any natural, non-fluffy material such as cotton or flannelette will also do this job efficiently, but avoid synthetic fibres such as nylon, rayon and terylene, as they do not absorb the polish effectively and are sometimes attacked by acetone when used to clean brushes.

Stirring sticks

For mixing of catalyst, pigment and fillers into the resin.

Sponges

Small 75 mm (3 in) blocks or cubes of foam rubber or natural sponge provide the most efficient method of applying PVA release agent to the mould. The sponge absorbs a reasonable quantity of the release agent and allows a very thin, even coverage to be applied to the mould with little risk of streaking, bubbling or drips.

Waste paper

Kitchen towelling or old newspapers are very useful in the GRP workshop for wiping resin from brushes and rollers, placing under small mouldings on the bench and covering the floor and other areas where resin spillage might cause damage. As with any messy hobby, moulding in GRP uses great amounts of paper between setting up the moulds and rubbing up the final polish.

PERSONAL SAFETY AND FIRST-AID EQUIPMENT

Protective clothing in the form of overalls, dustcoat or apron should be worn when working with GRP, together with old footwear. Care should be taken to keep this clothing well stowed away when not in use, as glassfibre dust contaminating it will cause considerable discomfort when next it is worn.

Barrier cream should be applied to the hands, wrists and forearms each time work is commenced. This cream protects the pores of the skin from fibreglass dust and also prevents drying out of the skin as a result of handling catalysts, resins and solvents. Thin, disposable PVC gloves give protection for a short period when laminating. But they soon get torn and so are of limited value on large lay-up jobs. They are particularly useful, however, when putting on a gelcoat or brushing-out coat.

Goggles and *mask* are necessary when drilling or grinding laminates as GRP dust tends to get in the eyes and, apart from being extremely painful, could cause eye damage. There is a variety of goggles and masks on the market ranging from the simple disposable paper equipment, through plastic masks containing a strip of foam rubber as a filter, to the sophisticated respirator mask containing replaceable gauze and paper filters. The type of mask and goggles used will obviously depend on the degree of grinding or drilling being done.

Safety first

Acetone is highly inflammable and MEKP readily supports combustion, so there is always an extreme fire risk in the GRP

A nose mask is essential when fine powdered GRP dust is in the air. Even hand sanding creates dangerous dust which can be inhaled. Goggles should also be used to protect the eyes.

workshop. The 'open cup' flash point of acetone is −9.4°C (15°F), MEKP 1.1°C (35°F), and styrene monomer 36.6°C (98°F). A foam type fire extinguisher and a fire blanket are, therefore, sensible investments but are no substitute for careful handling of the materials.

Water should always be available for washing hands, brushes and rollers and also to cool down any resin which might have become overheated during exotherm. Smoking in the workshop is, of course, *Verboten!*

First-aid

Apart from being flammable, MEKP is a highly corrosive peroxide and so contact with the skin should be avoided. Eyes are especially vulnerable to injury by MEKP, and should an accident occur, immediate thorough irrigation with water is essential. The eye should then be bathed with a dilute solution of sodium bicarbonate and medical help sought as quickly as possible. Resin in the eye is not so serious but is extremely painful. Water and cotton buds soaked in bicarbonate of soda should be used to remove all traces of the resin.

Cuts and abrasions are not uncommon in the GRP workshop. Such wounds should be washed thoroughly to avoid the risk of infection and adhesive strips used to seal them. Acetone will quickly dissolve adhesive strips and cause burning of any exposed wound, so extra care is required when working with chemicals if any cuts or skin damage are liable to be contaminated.

One of the most common and painful injuries sustained when working with GRP is getting a sliver of glassfibre embedded in the skin. Tweezers and needles are therefore essential items in the first-aid box. This type of injury is liable to become infected, so take care to remove the whole sliver in one piece if possible, wash the wound and apply antiseptic.

3 MOULDING IN FIBREGLASS

MOULDS

The GRP hand lay-up process normally requires the use of a female mould — that is, a mould with a smooth inside surface on which the gelcoat and glassfibre reinforcement are laid.

Hiring a mould

GRP moulds for popular items such as canoes, sailing dinghies, power boats, garden furniture, and car and motorbike accessories are sometimes available for hire. In the case of larger moulds such as those used for laying up yachts and swimming pools, technical assistance can also be hired. Moulds are usually hired by the week and the manufacturer frequently sells a 'kit' of materials along with the mould hire, sufficient to produce one moulding. This is probably the easiest and least expensive method of gaining experience in GRP moulding.

Buying a mould

Moulds can be made to order by GRP manufacturers or bought second hand. Both are expensive ways of acquiring a mould but the cost can sometimes be justified if the moulding is a popular product and a number of 'shells' can be pulled to recover the initial outlay. When hiring or purchasing a GRP mould always check the following points:

1 The condition of the working surface. Scratches, chips, crazing and pinholes will detract from the finish of a moulding. A poor mould surface may also create difficulties in releasing the lay-up when it is completed.
2 Whether the mould is 'true' or has warped since its construction. Inadequate glassfibre content or the lack of a suitable cradle or reinforcement can cause a mould to warp. Poor storage or exposure to excessive temperature changes

Male and female moulds. Female mould (top) gives a smooth exterior and rough moulded interior. Male mould (centre) produces smooth interior, rough exterior. To obtain a GRP reproduction of the silver plate (foreground), both male and female moulds are used. The finished product (right) is then smooth on both sides.

while the mould is still green can also alter the shape. Moulds should incorporate flanges along the edges whenever possible as this procedure helps retain the shape of the mould and also helps prevent damage to the mould edge when trimming. If a mould surface is black in colour, this probably indicates that it has been made using tooling gelcoat which gives a tougher, more resilient working surface than normal gelcoats. Tooling gelcoat can be worked up to a high polish and is more resistant to styrene attack during the lay-up of the moulding.

Frequently more than one mould is required to construct a GRP product. For instance, a dinghy may require hull,

Stiffeners bonded to the bottom of this surf-ski mould not only support it on the work bench, but also prevent the possibility of it warping out of shape.

The condition of the mould will affect the finish of the product. A very badly marked mould may prevent the moulding from releasing when cured.

gunwale, buoyancy chambers and seat moulds. A slalom kayak may incorporate deck, hull and seat and cockpit moulds. It is important to ensure that these moulds 'match up' as intended, otherwise it can be most frustrating and sometimes impossible to effect a join between mouldings.

Constructing a mould

Often it is not possible to purchase or hire a suitable mould in which case it will be necessary to build one. The GRP technique involved is different to the normal basic lay-up procedure and requires an original product or a built plug on which the mould can be constructed. Details of the construction of a mould are included later in this book.

Making a plug

If a completely new shape is to be created, the first step is to

A small boat mould can be built up using plywood or masonite. To achieve a good moulding, however, special treatment and a high degree of finish are necessary.

construct a suitable plug. The term 'plug' is given to the form or 'mock-up' shape from which the mould is taken. The construction of the plug is the most skilful part of the whole process and involves the use of a wide variety of materials — almost any material, in fact, which can be made to form the required shape. Timber battens, masonite sheet, wire mesh, hessian and plaster are usually employed in this work but other materials such as concrete, plasticine, tinplate and polythene sheeting may also be used. The object is to produce a shape whose external dimensions and surface finish are identical to the proposed moulding.

Many hours of painstaking work are required to produce an accurate, symmetrical plug with a high gloss finish. Flat surfaces such as the sides of a dinghy hull can be made from masonite sheets, while the curved surfaces of, say, a canoe will require the use of light mesh wire, paper packing and plaster. Details of plug construction are given later in this book. Once the plug has been accurately formed to the required shape and dimensions, a suitable finish must be applied so that a GRP mould can be laid-up on the surface of the plug.

There are two good finishes:

1 *Shellac varnish* is a suitable finish for a number of surfaces, particularly plaster. Shellac can be polished with mould release wax and does not react with polyester resin. Shellac varnish also fills and binds a delicate plaster surface and, having a methylated spirit base, is not adversely affected by any moisture in the plaster surface.

2 *Polyester flow coat resin*, containing 5 per cent wax in styrene. This is the most common treatment applied to a plug surface as it sets hard and can be cut back with wet or dry abrasive paper to remove brush marks and similar blemishes. It can also be treated with release wax and PVA in the normal manner. If used to seal a plaster plug, the plaster must be thoroughly dry or the resin will be 'thrown' from the surface in the form of wrinkles.

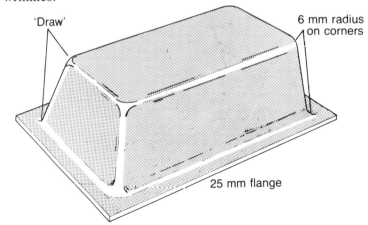

Illustrating the curve diameters and 'draw' of a well designed plug.

Due allowance must be made for 'draw' (mould release angles) when the plug is being designed. This means that shallow curves rather than sharp corners should be used where possible to make removal of the mould from the plug easy. Curves incorporated in the plug shape should not be of less than 6 mm (¼ in) radius, otherwise difficulty may be experienced in getting the CSM to lie tightly in the curves against the gelcoat. The natural 'spring' or resilience of the glassfibre may cause it to move away from the gelcoat layer resulting in an air pocket forming between gelcoat and the reinforcement layers. This fault can in turn cause unsightly pockets in the gelcoat surface of the completed mould.

Split moulds

If very tight corners, known as 'non-release' or 'non-return' angles are incorporated in the plug design then 'split' moulds will have to be constructed to allow for easy release of the mouldings.

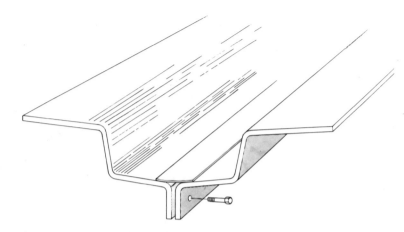

Illustrating the use of masking tape to cover the join between sides of a split mould.

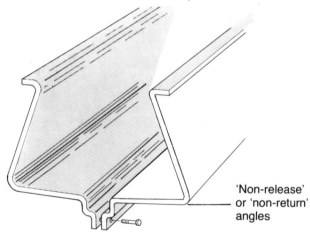

'Non-release' or 'non-return' angles

Whenever difficult angles, particularly 'non-release' angles, are concerned, a split mould is the only way of retrieving the moulding from the mould once the laminate has cured. Bolts along the bottom of the mould are released and both sides of the mould fall apart. This type of mould is particularly common with large yachts.

Moulds which can be unbolted and 'split' apart to allow release of the moulding are more difficult to make but give greater versatility of plug shape. Flanges are required at the joints of split moulds to provide an accurate method of bolting the two halves of the mould together and to help prevent warping of the moulds during cure.

It is good practice to cover the join or split between the moulds with adhesive tape or paper masking tape prior to application of the gelcoat. This eradicates the 'flashing' of gelcoat which would otherwise form between the moulds. A flashing takes time to remove from the finished moulding and sometimes even adheres to the flanges and bolts, making it difficult to release the moulding from the moulds.

Fabrication of a female or mock-up mould

Instead of building a plug, a 'mock-up' mould or 'female plug', with a smooth working surface on the inside, can be constructed using any suitable plug-making materials. This is an excellent procedure to follow if a one-off or prototype moulding is required,

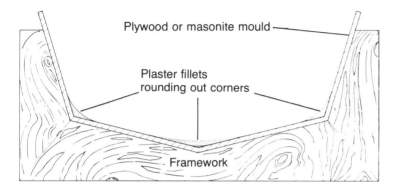

Plywood or masonite mould

Plaster fillets
rounding out corners

Framework

Cross section of a mock-up or fabricated mould. Plaster fillets round out the corners at chine and keel to provide more aesthetic shape and make the moulding easier to pull from the mould.

Steps in fabricating a small boat mould. The basic external framework is built from plans or drawings and sheets of plywood or masonite fastened into it to create the mould.

with the possibility of modification and changes being planned after testing.

The advantages of this type of mould are:

1 The time, materials and costs involved in normal plug construction can be applied to the fabrication of the mould itself.

2 No GRP female mould is required. The moulding can be laid up inside the 'mock-up' mould direct, thus saving the not inconsiderable cost of the female mould.

3 The moulding so produced can be used as 'plug' or 'male former' to produce a GRP female mould at a later date — perhaps after testing and modification of the prototype.

4 No draw is required on the 'mock-up' mould as it can easily be split or broken apart to 'release' the moulding. In this case, however, any subsequent GRP mould would have to be of the 'split' type to allow for release of the moulding.

Given the above list of advantages it would appear that there is no reason to struggle with the problems of fabricating a plug and

The 'shell' of the mould is built up. Nail holes and similar blemishes can be filled with plaster and faired back later.

Smoothing off the interior of the mould and filling blemishes is the most important part of the job or the finished moulding will show the imperfections and probably stick to the mould.

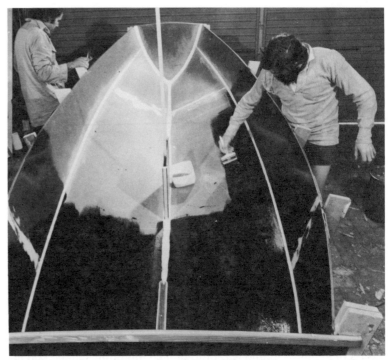

The final touches to ensure that the moulding will be as near perfect as possible. A coat of resin or shellac seals the surface which, after cure, is ready for waxing.

female mould in order to 'pop out' one GRP moulding. In some cases this is true but there are certain limitations to the 'mock-up' mould idea. Principally, these revolve around the difficulty in constructing the mould in all but simple shapes. If the mould is designed mainly to produce a product with mostly flat panels and generous radius curves then this method is ideal. If, however, considerable curves are involved then it would be very difficult to construct accurately the 'mock-up' mould.

BASIC HAND LAY-UP TECHNIQUES

Normally the work is carried out in a female mould — a GRP mould with a polished gelcoat surface on the inside. Having acquired and set up the mould at a convenient working height in the workshop, the following procedure should be adopted:

1 Wash the mould carefully with warm water and soft soap to remove any old PVA release agent, dust, grease, finger marks, etc.

2 Dry the mould thoroughly.

3 Check the mould surface for chips or blemishes. These should be repaired by filling with polyester filler and cutting back with wet and dry paper. The odd small chip can be temporarily repaired by filling with plasticine or plaster filler.

4 If the mould surface is in good condition the mould release wax is now applied, with a circular action, using a small piece of cloth. One coat of wax is sufficient for a mould surface which has been previously 'broken in' but a new mould surface will require at least six applications. Each application is polished up to a high shine with a large piece of cheesecloth, after being left to harden for 15-20 minutes. Care must be taken to remove all streaks of wax from the mould surface. Polishing is correctly done when there is no sticking or pulling of the cloth when it is rubbed over the mould surface.

5 Apply the polyvinyl alcohol solution carefully with a piece of sponge or foam rubber. Some PVA solutions are coloured (say green or red) to assist in getting an even and complete coverage, but if the PVA is applied 'against the light' and you work progressively from one end of the mould, you should have no problems. Avoid going over the mould surface more than once with the sponge as this may lift the layer of PVA previously applied. PVA solution contains water and so must be allowed to dry completely before the gelcoat is applied. At normal room temperature (approximately 21°C (70°F)) this takes about 15 minutes.

6 The gelcoat is now weighed out, the pigment mixed into it and

Every tiny mark on the mould will be exaggerated on the moulding, so careful checking and repair of the mould is essential before laying-up.

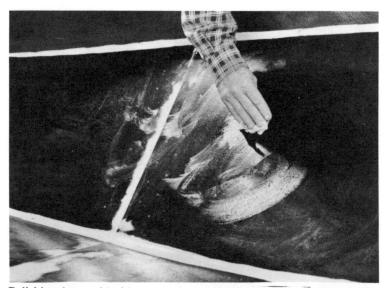

Polishing the mould with a carnauba wax is a laborious but rewarding task. A circular action rubs the wax hard into the mould surface, filling small blemishes and allowing easy release of the finished product.

A heavy, thick coating of the gelcoat ensures good coverage. Brushing with strokes in one direction only helps to spread the coat evenly.

the correct quantity of catalyst stirred in. In industry the gelcoat is frequently sprayed onto the mould surface or applied with large lambswool rollers. For amateur use, however, a soft bristle (50-120 mm (2-5 in) brush is the most suitable. Care must be taken to ensure an even coverage of gelcoat resin, free from blobs, deep ridges, shallow furrows and air bubbles.

Practice makes perfect and very quickly you will learn to work from one end of the mould, spreading the gel with light, even strokes *in one direction only*. Vigorous 'painting' strokes give too thin a gel coverage and can sometimes cause the PVA to lift from the mould surface. The gelcoat surface is applied very thickly compared to a painted surface. To avoid serious gelcoat problems, it is safer to err on the slightly heavy side, rather than apply too thin a coating.

The gelcoat should have as short a pot life as possible, within reason (say about 10-15 minutes), as lengthy geltime on the mould allows excessive evaporation of the styrene monomer and this could result in permanent undercure of the gelcoat. Also a long gellation period can allow the styrene to attack the mould surface and cause a polystyrene build-up. This will spoil the highly polished appearance of both the mould and the moulding.

Ideally, the lay-up of the fibreglass reinforcement should commence as soon as the gelcoat has cured sufficiently to be hard to the touch. This stage of cure may take from one to four hours depending on such factors as catalyst levels, working temperature, humidity and mould shape. One test is to touch the *lowest* point in the mould gently with the fingertip. The gelcoat should feel slightly 'tacky' but solid, and no pigmentation should come off on the finger. Another useful test is to rub gently this part of the mould with a rag dipped in acetone. Slight pigmentation will be removed from the tacky surface but no softening of the gelcoat film should occur. The lowest point in the mould is used as an indicator since this is the last part to cure.

It is important to note that gelcoats are normally 'air inhibited', that is, they remain slightly 'tacky' during cure so that a good chemical bond can be established between the gelcoat and the first glassfibre reinforcement layer. While the gelcoat should not be allowed to overcure, it is equally important that the lay-up of the polyester resin and glassfibre reinforcement should not be commenced until the gelcoat has reached the stage mentioned above, otherwise the styrene in the polyester resin will soften and wrinkle the gelcoat, causing unsightly blemishes in the finished moulding.

Leaving the gelcoat on the mould for too long a period prior to lay-up of the reinforcement material may cause the useful tacky period of the cure to be lost. At the same time, dust, grit and moisture (humidity) deposits, which could affect adversely the bonding of gelcoat to laminate, may settle on the surface. If a mould must be left for a period of hours after gelcoat application it should be placed under a polythene 'tent' or, in the case of a small mould, in a cupboard or possibly inverted by suspending it from a wire. If it is not possible to apply the laminating resin for some time, adhesion between gelcoat and laminate can be improved by giving the gelcoat surface a thorough acetone wash prior to the glassfibre lay-up. It is essential to dry off all acetone before applying the laminating resin.

Laying up a GRP moulding

After the gelcoat has cured, the moulding is reinforced by bonding some form of glassfibre reinforcement to the gelcoat with polyester laminating resin. In amateur mouldings the glass usually takes the form of chopped strand mat because of the cost and ease of application. However, tissues, tapes, woven rovings and cloths may also be used and each will impart specific strength and

The CSM is cut slightly over size using careful measurements on templates to obtain the right shapes. Over or under cutting the mat at this stage can ruin the job.

Hanging the pre-cut sheets of CSM will prevent them kinking or tearing. Cutting most of the required shapes beforehand avoids delays during the lay-up when the resin may start to cure and thus weaken the laminate.

performance factors to the moulding. Since the lay-up technique is the same for all types of reinforcement, we shall deal here with the more common CSM.

The glassfibre required for the lay-up should have been previously cut to the shape of the mould by means of plywood templates, paper patterns or by approximate measurements taken directly from the mould. A steel tape measure is useful here as it can be easily flexed to follow the contours of the mould and then laid out on the cutting table and used as a straight edge. The CSM should be cut so that, when placed in the mould, it should not extend beyond the edge of the mould by more than about 25 mm (1 in), otherwise the excess material may sag when wet and pull the mould material away from the surface, leaving an air cavity between mat and gelcoat.

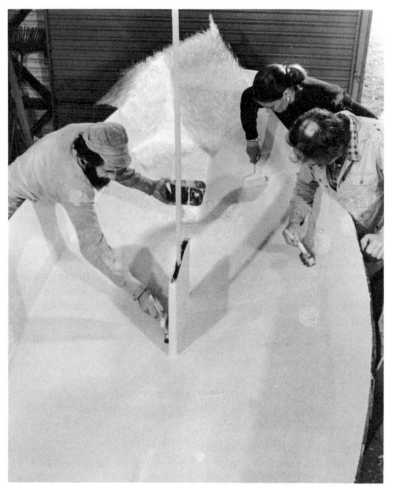

Smooth, swift work is the keynote to laying up. As the first coat of resin is placed on the gelcoat, the first sheet of CSM is placed onto it and carefully positioned. The second coat of resin should follow immediately and be thoroughly worked through the mat.

Where difficult corners are encountered or where thinner layers of mat are required, the CSM can be 'teased' apart. With woven cloth it must be cut, which creates a severe edge and is not as satisfactory.

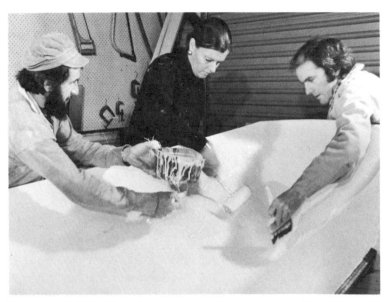

It's a case of all hands to the pumps once the mat is in position. Thorough wetting out with brushes and lambswool rollers ensures good saturation through the mat. Vaned rollers later compress the newly laid laminate and drive out air bubbles.

The lay-up takes place in the following stages:

1 The laminating resin is weighed out, pigmented to match the gelcoat (if desired) and then catalysed.
2 A brush or roller is used to apply a liberal coating of resin to the gelcoat surface.
3 A shaped layer of CSM is placed carefully in the mould and the previously applied resin worked through it. Additional resin is applied to the CSM surface at this stage and all fibres are stippled or rolled until thoroughly and evenly 'wetted out' with resin.

The first layer is very important as it reinforces the gelcoat and prevents air pockets from forming behind it. For this reason a layer of surface tissue or a thin layer of CSM is often laid up first. In the case of small mouldings, the standard 445 gm/m² (1½ oz/ft²) mat can be teased apart into two separate layers. This ensures that the CSM will not pull out of tight corners or uneven spots in the gelcoat. In most amateur work, however, tight corners should be avoided and moulds with large radius curves used. In this case the standard weight CSM can be successfully used for the initial lay-up.

4 A second layer of CSM is applied as soon as the first is thoroughly wetted out and as much resin as possible is stippled through the mat from the previous layer. Additional resin is added sparingly by brush, the object being to achieve a

Overlap on the edges of the mould is kept to a minimum to avoid the wet laminate sagging out of shape.

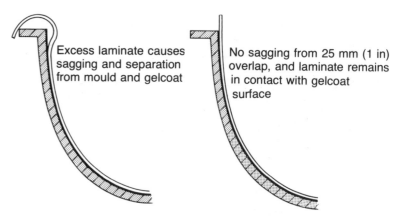

Excess laminate causes sagging and separation from mould and gelcoat

No sagging from 25 mm (1 in) overlap, and laminate remains in contact with gelcoat surface

Illustrating the problems caused by excess overlap of wet laminate.

thorough wet out of the CSM with the minimum quantity of resin.

5 Immediately after the second layer of CSM has been applied a compression roller (washer or vane type) is used to compress the mat and squeeze air bubbles and excess resin from the laminate. This technique appreciably improves the strength of the moulding by increasing its density and reducing its porosity on the inside surface, so it is important that the rollers are used firmly and evenly across the entire surface.

6 Successive layers of laminate are now applied to the mould until the lay-up is complete. Each layer is compression rolled as described above. The number of layers required will depend on the type of moulding and the structural stresses it will need to withstand in use.

7 When the resin in the lay-up has polymerised sufficiently to allow the laminate to be trimmed with a Stanley knife or plane blade the cure has reached what is known as the 'toffee' stage. This is the ideal time to trim all edges and usually lasts for about 15-20 minutes. If trimming is delayed until the initial cure is

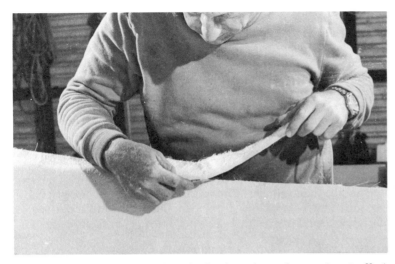

Careful trimming of edges when the laminate is partly cured — 'toffee' stage — can eliminate a lot of hard cutting later.

complete a coping saw and surform file will be required. This is hard work and often takes more time than that involved in the actual lay-up. Trimming at the 'toffee' stage, on the other hand, is the work of only a few minutes and if done carefully gives a clean, precise cut along the edge of the mould. At the same time excess gel from the flange of the mould is also removed. The only further edge treatment required then is a rub with garnet paper *after* the moulding has been pulled from the mould.

Notes on lay-up techniques

The glassfibre laminate used in any GRP moulding can be made up from different types of glassfibre material depending on the specific function of the end product. For example, woven rovings add bulk and therefore rigidity to a moulding. Finely woven glassfibre and nylon cloths create flexibility and resilience. Chopped strand mat gives a multi-directional rigidity, while continuous roving filaments give uni-directional strength as

required in vaulting poles. Woven glassfibre cloth and tape can be soaked in resin and wound round a mandrel to give a hollow tube (filament wound laminate) with great axial strength as used for fishing rods, radio aerials and yacht masts.

Any GRP laminate will generate heat during the polymerisation of the resin so it is important to limit the thickness of the lay-up to 4 or 5 layers of 445 gm/m^2 (1½ oz/ft^2) CSM or equivalent at a time. Otherwise, there will be a risk of overheating the moulding which could result in warping and weakening of the finished product. Even more importantly, perhaps, there is a risk of damage to the mould surface due to excessive heat build-up.

In addition to the reinforcing used in normal lamination, a GRP moulding can be further reinforced at specific points simply by increasing the thickness of the reinforcement material during the lay-up procedure. Overlapping two sheets of CSM on a corner, for example, offers twice the thickness and thus greatly increased strength at that point. Additional reinforcement can be added by using a wide range of materials which are moulded into the job after the initial lay-up has cured. Some of these materials are:

Strip strengthening materials

These can be in the form of timber, carbon fibre or polyurethane foam strips, cardboard or plastic tubes, papier mâché, rope, etc. These materials, when bonded onto the inside surface of the

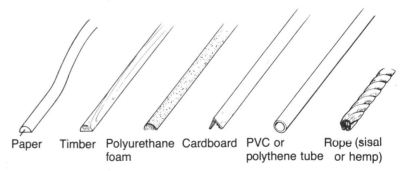

Paper   Timber   Polyurethane   Cardboard   PVC or   Rope (sisal
             foam   polythene tube   or hemp)

Typical materials used as cores for GRP strip strengthening overlays.

Rolled newspaper bonded into place with a layer of CSM makes ideal cheap reinforcing material and is widely used on small craft.

cured laminate act as corrugations and as such give the moulding rigidity with minimum weight gain. When weight gain is critical, tubes of polythene can be used for this purpose and pulled out of the mould when the overlay of glassfibre has reached the 'toffee' stage.

Area strengthening materials

These usually consist of polyurethane foam or end grain balsa used as sandwich reinforcement. They give strength, in the form of rigidity, to large areas of a moulding with a minimum of weight gain. They also help to keep GRP costs down. These materials are normally obtainable in sheet form on a flexible backing so that they can be made to follow the contours of the moulding. They are glued onto the inside of the cured laminate with polyester resin and then sealed over with 1 or 2 layers of GRP.

Fastenings

These are generally metal or timber fittings which are bonded into a GRP laminate either before or after removal from the mould. If possible, total cure of 28 days should be allowed before heavy, localised fittings are bonded into a moulding, as there is a risk of local shrinkage of the bonding laminate layers. This creates a 'print through' on the gelcoat side of the moulding, which appears as an indentation on the otherwise smooth gelcoat following the contours of the fitting. It looks unsightly and in extreme cases can cause cracking of the gelcoat and weakening of the laminate layers of the moulding.

Woven rovings and heavy gauge glassfibre cloths can 'telegraph' their patterns through to the surface of the gelcoat if not sufficiently 'insulated' from it by the use of surface tissue or chopped strand mat. This is another form of 'print through'.

Pulling the moulding from the mould

In industry, compressed air or pressurised water is sometimes used between mould and moulding to help release mouldings with deep 'draw' from the mould. Nozzles are embedded in the bottom of the mould and covered with tape or a plug of plasticine before gelcoat lay-up commences, and the moulding is 'floated' or 'popped' out of the mould on completion. Split moulds are also used where difficult shaped mouldings are made. The mould is in two halves which can be unbolted and easily levered apart, thus 'cracking' the moulding clear of the mould.

In the home workshop, however, these methods are usually neither practical nor necessary. Shallow moulds, with reasonable 'draw', and which are slightly flexible should be used and the moulding released by flexing gently. Slight twist may also be applied to the mould to help break the bond and as a rule this is the only effort required to 'crack' out a shallow moulding, provided it has been correctly trimmed to the edge of the mould and the release agents have been properly applied.

Flexing the mould will 'start' the moulding at one or two points and strips of soft plywood or masonite can then be wedged

The critical moment — releasing the moulding from the mould. If the preparation of the mould surface was adequate before moulding, then slight flexing of the product should 'crack' it clear of the mould.

between mould and moulding. The wedges are then carefully pulled along the top edge of the moulding until it is released from the mould all round. If need be, the strips can then be pressed further down round the contours of the mould until total release is obtained. Under no circumstances should chisels, screwdrivers or plane blades be used to wedge or lever the moulding from the mould. This will result in scratching or even chipping of the mould and would ruin it for future mouldings.

The moulding should be left to cure for as long as possible in its mould — total cure takes about 28 days, although most mouldings are rigid enough to resist warping after 24 hours. If, however, the moulding has a tendency to flop or sag slightly after removal from the mould, it should be supported in some way to prevent permanent distortion during further curing.

Flow coating

After all reinforcements (if any) have been bonded into the moulding the inside surface is usually rubbed down with 80 grit garnet paper to remove any sharp fibres, the dust is removed and a 'flow coat' applied to the laminate. The flow coat is polyester resin containing about 5 per cent paraffin wax dissolved in styrene. The functions of a flow coat are:

1 To seal the laminate surface from attack by moisture, grit, grease, chemicals, etc.
2 To remove the 'tacky' feel from the laminating resin used in the lay-up
3 To give the moulding a clean internal finish with colour uniformity, if desired.

The wax floats to the surface of the flow coat and prevents air inhibition of the resin cure which would leave the surface tacky. The result is a hard, shiny surface free from porosity and sharp fibres.

Decorative effects in the gelcoat

Flashings, name blocks and similar decorative patterns can be inlaid during the gelcoat lay-up rather than being spray or hand

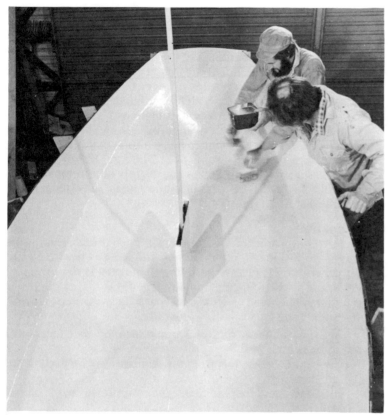

Decorative stripes and insignia can add a great deal to the appearance of a moulding and are quite easy to achieve.

Just as a coat of paint adds finish to an external surface, so the flow coat gives a good finish to the rough moulded interior. In addition to cosmetic finishing, the flow coat also forms a hard, firm surface over the 'tacky' surface of the laminate.

painted on the surface of the finished moulding. These markings are popular in leisure craft and equipment and are easily applied to a mould at the gelcoat stage. This technique does, however, require a particular procedure, and a very steady hand. After thorough waxing and polishing of the mould area to be decorated, masking tape or cellophane tape is used to mark out the shape of the required decoration. The appropriately coloured gelcoat is then carefully applied and the tape is then immediately stripped off while the gelcoat is still liquid. If the gelcoat should begin to polymerise before the tape is removed the work will be spoiled as subsequent removal of the tape will lift the edge of the gelcoat. Any drips or brush marks which land on the mould surface outside the taped area should be allowed to polymerise and then chipped off with a finger nail. No attempt should be made to wipe off any resin marks while they are still wet as this will only spread the resin or, if acetone is used, will remove the wax protection from the mould surface.

Note: PVA solution cannot be used under the taped areas as removal of the tape will lift the PVA coating which, in turn, will cause the edge of the wet gelcoat to peel off the mould and spoil the sharp definition of the pattern.

4 BUILDING SMALL CRAFT IN FIBREGLASS

BUILDING A SLALOM CANOE

Refer to the tools and the equipment lists and lay-up procedures mentioned previously. Three moulds are normally required — deck, hull, cockpit seat and coaming.

Gelcoat application

1 Wash, dry, wax and polish the three moulds. If decorative effects are to be inlaid, these should now be taped out on the mould surface and the coloured gelcoat applied.

2 Apply PVA release agent to entire surface except taped areas and allow 15-20 minutes drying time.

3 Measure out enough gelcoat resin to cover the hull mould, stir in pigment paste and finally add the correct quantity of catalyst (refer to the chart for catalyst quantities, room temperatures and working times).

MATERIALS REQUIRED TO MOULD A SLALOM CANOE
Length 4.5 m (15 ft) x beam 600 mm (2 ft)

(Metric measures)

Parts	Gelcoat kg	Lam. resin kg	CSM 445 gm/m² metres²	No. of layers	Additional materials
Deck	1¼	5	5	2	
Hull	1¼	5	5	2	
Seat and Coaming	¼	1½	1½	Coaming 2 Seat 4	
Reinforcement in hull		1	1	2	Any suitable core material
Flowcoat deck and hull		½			
Joining deck and hull		2	2	2	
Buoyancy					2 x 250 ml pack PU foam ¼ kg potch
Joining coaming to deck					

(Imperial measures)

Parts	Gelcoat lb	Lam. resin lb	CSM 1½ oz/ft² Feet²	No. of layers	Additional materials
Deck	2.5	11	52	2	
Hull	2.5	11	52	2	
Seat and Coaming	0.5	3.5	16	Coaming 2 Seat 4	
Reinforcement in hull		2			
Flowcoat deck and hull		1			
Joining deck and hull		4.5	21	2	
Buoyancy					2 x 250 ml pack of PU foam 0.5 lb potch
Joining coaming to deck					

4 Immediately apply the gelcoat to the mould, brushing consistently in one direction.
5 On completion, clean brushes in acetone.
6 Repeat the procedure with deck and seat moulds using the appropriate pigmentation.

Laying up the laminate

1 Check mould and ensure that the gelcoat has completed its initial cure.
2 Measure out a reasonable working quantity of laminating resin (say 2 kg (4½ lb)), stir in pigment paste to make the required colour and add the correct quantity of catalyst.
3 Using brush or lambswool roller apply a generous coating of laminating resin to the gelcoat surface.
4 Apply the first layer of CSM and soak thoroughly with resin using a wide brush or lambswool roller and 'painting' the resin on.
5 Apply the second layer of CSM and force as much resin as possible through the laminate using brush or roller. Apply more resin sparingly until the laminate is fully 'wetted out'.
6 Use the compression roller gently over the whole mould surface to compress the laminate and force out any trapped air.
7 Allow the lay-up to polymerise to the 'toffee' stage and then trim the edges with a Stanley knife or plane blade. Repeat the procedure with deck and seat/coaming moulds. *Note:* The base and sides of the seat moulding require four layers of 445 gm/m^2 (1½ oz/ft^2) CSM to give the necessary strength and rigidity.
8 After a 24-hour cure period a reinforcement corrugation — approximately 3 m (10 ft) long x 2 layers of 445 gm/m^2 (1½ oz/ft^2) CSM — is laid up along the centre of the hull. A number of materials are available for use as a core for the corrugation.
9 After cure the laminated surface of each moulding is lightly sanded down to remove any sharp protruding fibres and a flow coat is applied. The deck and hull mouldings should be flow coated only to within 75 mm (3 in) of their edges. This ensures

a good bond when applying the strips of CSM over the join. The join can be bonded while the mouldings are still in their moulds, or after release.

Bonding the hull mouldings together

1. *In the mould*

The deck and hull moulds are bolted together so that the mouldings form a butt joint at the gunwale. The whole assembly is now either slung from the roof — with the cockpit on its side — at a convenient working height, or placed on edge, on a table, against a wall. Joining the gunwale edges of the mouldings by laying strips of resin-impregnated CSM on the inside surface, is the most difficult part of the canoe construction, and is a technique which can only be mastered with practice.

The following pieces of equipment will be of use:
An inspection lamp.
A 30 mm (1 3/16 in) brush attached to handle long enough to reach the bow of the canoe from the cockpit.
A worktop covered with polythene sheeting on which to 'wet out' the joining strips of CSM.

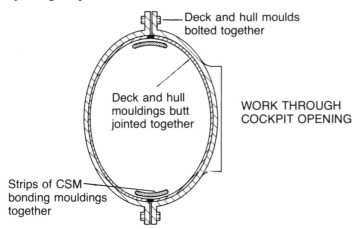

— Deck and hull moulds bolted together

Deck and hull mouldings butt jointed together

WORK THROUGH COCKPIT OPENING

Strips of CSM bonding mouldings together

Bonding hull and deck while still in the moulds.

In addition to overalls or dustcoat some form of hair protection is also required.
The procedure is as follows:

1 Cut enough strips of 445 gm/m² (1½ oz/ft²) CSM from the roll to run round the join twice. The strips of CSM should be about 100 mm (4 in) wide.
2 Coat or 'brush out' the surface on either side of the join from the cockpit to the bow, using laminating resin.
3 'Wet out' a 300 mm (12 in) strip of CSM on the workbench, lay it over the brush head and rest it along the handle.
4 Gently manoeuvre the long handled brush up the inside of the canoe until it touches the bow, then turn the handle upside down so the pre-soaked strip of CSM falls neatly over the join.
5 The joining strip is now gently 'stippled' down to remove any air blisters and the process is repeated, allowing an overlap of 50 mm (2 in) between strips. The area within reach of the cockpit can be worked with a 125 mm (5 in) laminating brush. The join must be covered with two layers of 445 gm/m² (1½ oz/ft²) CSM to give it the same minimum strength as the hull lay-up.
6 When the work on one side of the canoe has been completed the whole assembly is inverted and the joining procedure repeated. After 24-hours cure time the bolts are removed and the moulds prized apart by pushing a plane blade between the flange edges, and levering gently.

2 *Out of the mould*

The disadvantage of this method is that the green mouldings may 'flop' (alter their shape slightly) while being held in place ready for bonding. Also if they are allowed to cure out of the moulds, warping may take place, making it more difficult to achieve a perfect butt join between hull and deck.

On the credit side, however, this method has the advantage of allowing the moulds to be used again more quickly for a second lay-up. Also it occasionally happens that the moulding releases itself from the mould in places round the gunwale, leaving a gap which can be as wide as 5 mm (3/16 in). There are various reasons

Bonding deck and hull with wetted strips of CSM through the cockpit opening is the easiest and most common method for most small craft. The smaller cockpit openings of canoes can make the job fairly arduous.

for this — thick lay-up, tight curves or a hot resin mix causing excessive contraction of the laminating resin during cure. This means that the two halves of the moulding cannot be perfectly aligned in the moulds and after joining will be unsightly. Also in the course of laminating the join, resin will run into the gaps between the mould and the moulding, making for extra cleaning problems before the moulds can be re-used.

The problem can usually be overcome, however, by using the GRP materials correctly during the lay-up or by bonding the mouldings as soon as possible after the initial cure. If the mouldings are to be bonded after release from the moulds, one of two methods can be adopted to hold them together during lay-up of the joining strips.

Strips of CSM around 100 mm (4 in) wide being prepared for bonding hull and deck together.

Method 1 Paper masking tape or PVC floor marking tape is used to seal the join right round the canoe, and short vertical strips of tape maintain tension on the butt joint and keep both 'skins' of the canoe in alignment. The craft is now positioned and bonded exactly as described previously.

Method 2 If the two 'skins' have warped slightly during cure and will not come into alignment by means of tape, a 'fish-plate' system of forcing the two halves of the moulding together must be used. Usually only short lengths of the gunwale edges will require to be pulled into alignment using 'fish-plates', tape being used on those areas which butt together correctly. The procedure is as follows:

1 Bring the mould edges together and establish where misalignment occurs.
2 Using a felt tip pen mark the extremities of these areas (i.e. the points where the mould edges cross when laid one on top of the other).

3 Divide these marked lengths of the gunwale into, say, 200 mm (8 in) portions with the felt tip pen, marking both deck and hull at the same time.
4 File a small 'V' shape out of the deck and hull mouldings at the above points so that a No. 8 self-tapping screw can fit between the edges when they are touching.
5 Make-up the required number of pairs of 'plates' out of 8 mm (5/16 in) plywood and balance them by their respective screws in each slot. A clearance hole should be drilled in the outside pieces of plywood, while the inside 'plates' should be core drilled, threaded and waxed to allow easy 'take-up'.
6 Bring the two mouldings together and tape those areas which align themselves correctly. Check that all 'fish-plates' are in position and then, while pressing the two edges together, screw up the plates thus squeezing the mouldings into alignment.
7 Check that both mouldings are touching right round the gunwale and then seal the join with masking tape on the outside.

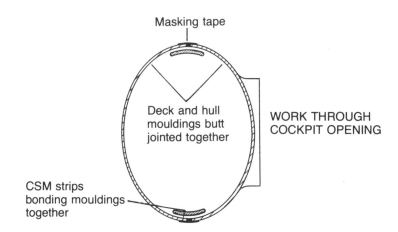

Bonding deck and hull out of the moulds.

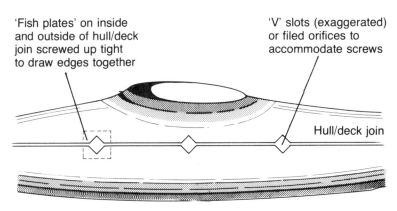

Plywood, cut-outs or 'fish plates' placed on either side of the hull/deck join pull together distortions between the edges when screwed up tight.

8 Set the canoe up as described previously and lay-up two layers of CSM over as much of the join as possible but being careful to keep clear of the plywood strips.

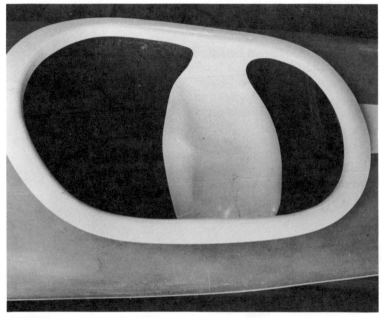

A typical cockpit seat and coaming moulding for a slalom canoe.

9 After cure the plates are removed, tape is applied over these areas on the outside and the laminating work is completed.

Attaching the coaming to the deck moulding
1 The cockpit opening in the deck is filed until the seat moulding can be pressed into position.
2 Masking tape is used to secure the coaming to the outside of the

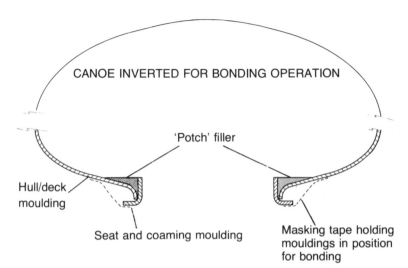

CANOE INVERTED FOR BONDING OPERATION

'Potch' filler

Hull/deck moulding

Seat and coaming moulding

Masking tape holding mouldings in position for bonding

The canoe must be inverted so that the resin filler used for bonding cockpit and hull mouldings together does not run out while curing.

deck. If it tends to 'spring' off the deck it may have to be temporarily secured in place using two small self-tapping screws. The screw holes can easily be filled with matching gelcoat resin after the bonding material has cured.
3 The canoe is inverted and supported fore and aft of the cockpit at a suitable working height.
4 ½ kg (1 lb) of potch is mixed up and applied between the edge of the coaming and the underside of the deck using a spatula knife. The sides of the seat are also potched to the underside of the deck so that a perfect seal is formed right round the coaming.
5 When the potch has gelled it is thoroughly sanded down with 80 grit garnet paper to remove any sharp points.
6 The seat is then bonded to the hull corrugation with CSM to help prevent hull flexing and seat 'wobble' during use.

Finishing the hull/deck join

The three most common methods of finishing off the outside edge of the deck and hull joint are:

PVC or 'magnetic' tapes.
Polyurethane paint strip.
Thixotropic resin strip.

As a prerequisite to all these methods, gelcoat 'flashings' should be removed from the joint by file and any gaps in the join line filled with a polyester filler. The canoe is then washed to remove the PVA coating, particularly from the area of the join.

PVC tapes are only a temporary covering but are quick and easy to apply. They look good and can easily be replaced when torn or worn.

With the polyurethane paint or thixotropic resin, the narrow strip to be painted or resin coated is 'masked off' with cellophane or paper tape and another length of tape is carefully butted along each side. The central strip of tape is then removed leaving the area to be treated suitably marked out. Use 230 grit silicon carbide paper to cut back the area inside the tape strips until the glaze and wax coating have been completely removed.

The canoe is then propped up against a wall with one edge on the floor, and the upper gunwale edge is carefully painted with appropriately coloured thixotropic resin or polyurethane lacquer. Normally a contrasting colour is used to accentuate the lines of the canoe. A small, soft bristle brush should be used to apply the coating so that brush marks can be avoided. If thixotropic resin is used a little wax in styrene should be added, along with the pigment and catalyst, to give a 'hard' non-tacky cure. Bear in mind that speed of application is important as the masking tape must be removed before the resin begins to 'gel'.

Buoyancy

A buoyancy system is essential in all GRP craft because the specific gravity of most GRP laminates is approximately 1.4 (specific gravity of fresh water is 1.0) and so, if swamped, the GRP craft will sink. The simplest buoyancy to install in a canoe is an expanded polyurethane foam system, which is mixed and poured directly into the areas where it is required. The foam sticks very firmly to the GRP laminate surface and so requires no further treatment to keep it in place.

The foam system consists of two liquid components which, when mixed in equal quantity, react vigorously and expand to form a chocolate coloured, closed cell foam. The volume of the mixture, if stirred thoroughly in warm conditions, increases 30 times in approximately 2 minutes. Thus the 2 x 250 ml (9 fl oz) pack will produce approximately 0.03 m^3 (1 ft^3) of foam — 13 300 cm^3 (½ ft^3) in each end of the canoe — more than adequate to support the combined weight of the canoe and the canoeist, when swamped.

The buoyancy must be evenly placed fore and aft of the cockpit so that the craft will lie horizontally in the water when awash, and not form a vertical 'needle' — a difficult position from which to recover.

When pouring polyurethane foam you will need two clean containers such as rimless tins or polyvinyl ice-cream containers. A power drill fitted with a small paint stirrer and a stool, box or ladder so that the foam can be poured into the canoe from the cockpit aperture when the craft is standing vertically against a wall.

The procedure is as follows:

1 Pour exactly half the contents of each tin into the mixing container.
2 Without delay, stir the contents vigorously with the power drill for 30 seconds.
3 Immediately pour the expanding mixture into the end of the canoe by stretching down inside the canoe, through the cockpit aperture, so that the foam is splashed about as little as possible.
4 After about 5 minutes the canoe can be safely up-ended and the same procedure repeated, using the balance of the foam mixture in the other end of the hull.

Caution: The fumes given off during expansion of the foam are toxic and should not be inhaled. The foaming operation should be

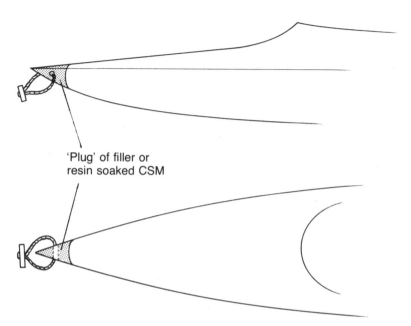

'Plug' of filler or
resin soaked CSM

A plug of filler or resin saturated CSM ensures good strength at the lifting points of the toggles. This should be fitted before buoyancy foam is poured in.

undertaken outside, or in a well-ventilated room.

The canoe construction is now complete but in the interests of safety and convenience a wooden toggle should be secured to both ends of the canoe by means of a short length of rope. This is done by drilling a 10 mm (⅜ in) hole horizontally through the hull about 25 mm (1 in) from the stem, and another 25 mm (1 in) from the stern. These holes cannot cause leakage as the foam buoyancy has completely sealed off both ends of the craft. Short lengths of nylon rope are threaded through both holes in the hull, forced through holes drilled in the toggles and 'burned off' to lock them in place.

BUILDING A CANADIAN CANOE

MATERIALS REQUIRED TO MOULD A CANADIAN CANOE
Length 5 m (17 ft) x beam 900 mm (3 ft)
(Metric measures)

Part	Gelcoat kg	Lam. resin kg	CSM 445 gm/m^2) Metres^2	No. of layers	Additional materials
Hull	2	10	10	2	Buoyancy. Either PU foam or sealed air tanks
Gunwale/seat moulding	1½	8	8	2	
Joining: Hull to gunwale Seat flanges to hull		2	2	2	
Hull reinforcement		2	2	2	PU foam, timber or cardboard core material
Seat reinforcement		1.5	1.5	2	
Flow coat		0.5			Bow and stern lifting toggles Nylon drain plugs for buoyancy chambers

(Imperial measures)

Part	Gelcoat lb	Lam. resin lb	CSM 1½ oz/ft² Feet²	No. of layers	Additional materials
Hull	4.5	22	105	2	Buoyancy. Either PU foam or sealed air tanks
Gunwale/seat moulding	3.5	18	84	2	
Joining: Hull to gunwale Seat flanges to hull		4.5	21	2	
Hull reinforcement		4.5	21	2	PU foam, timber or cardboard, core material
Seat reinforcement		3.5	16	2	
Flow coat		1			Bow and stern lifting toggles. Nylon drain plugs for buoyancy chambers

Two moulds are normally used — the hull mould and a second mould comprising sidedecks, coaming, seats and stern decking. A number of variations of the basic moulds may be available. One system uses two matching hull moulds, split along the centreline with a seat/coaming/sidedeck moulding or separate seat moulds. Another involves a single hull mould, with separate coaming and seat moulds.

Construction

All stages in the construction of the mouldings for this canoe are identical to those described earlier for the slalom canoe.

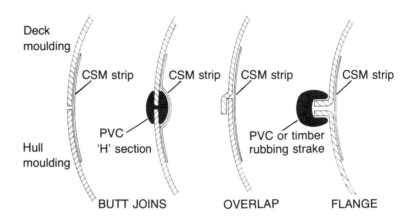

BUTT JOINS   OVERLAP   FLANGE

Because moulds differ, methods of bonding deck to hull may vary considerably. Illustrated are four different systems.

Joining

The joint between the hull and deck of a Canadian canoe can be butted, overlapped or flanged. Sometimes an 'H' section PVC strip is used to cover and finish off the butt joint. The flanged edge is usually covered with a PVC or timber moulding to protect the user's legs from injury when getting in and out. In all these joining methods the two mouldings are laminated on the inside using strips of CSM in the normal manner. In the case of the hull/coaming overlap joint the procedure is as follows:

1 Remove both mouldings from their respective moulds.
2 File and sandpaper the edges thoroughly and fit the two mouldings together.
3 Either: (a) Use pop-rivets or stainless steel self-tapping screws to secure the joint in the correct position, seal the joint on the outside using masking tape and then laminate the mouldings together on the inside, in the normal manner, or:
   (b) Use folding wedges to hold the joint in the correct position. Potch or laminate those areas of the joint between the

wedges. After cure the wedges are removed and the exposed areas bonded.

Seats
These are usually either an integral part of the sidedeck moulding, or made out of timber and screwed to stringers which are suitably bonded to the inside of the hull. They may also be separate GRP mouldings which are designed to fit against the hull at specific points. These normally include flanged edges which are overlaid with CSM and thus laminated to the hull. Frequently, they also form sealed buoyancy chambers.

Buoyancy
Polyurethane foam buoyancy is usually poured into the bow and stern, under the short decked areas. Blocks of polyurethane foam may also be used by shaping them to fit bow and stern and under

the thwarts. Polyurethane foam can be laminated directly to the canoe structure if desired. *Note:* Polystyrene foam cannot be used in this way as it is instantly attacked and dissolved by the styrene in the polyester resin, and so cannot be glassed into position.

Rigidity
The hull of a Canadian canoe with, say, three persons aboard is subjected to large and variable stress loadings and so must be designed to withstand them.

This is done by a combination of the methods listed:

1 Increasing the thickness of the hull laminate lay-up.
2 A keel and/or bilge keels moulded into the hull shape.
3 Reinforcement corrugations of GRP laminated into the hull after lay-up and cure.
4 The use of internal fittings such as seats and buoyancy chambers which are laminated to the hull.

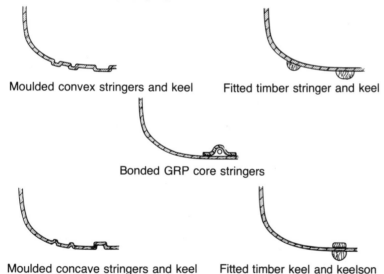

Moulded convex stringers and keel   Fitted timber stringer and keel

Bonded GRP core stringers

Moulded concave stringers and keel   Fitted timber keel and keelson

Some methods of attaining hull bottom rigidity in GRP canoes.

52

BUILDING A SURF-SKI

MATERIALS REQUIRED TO MOULD A SURF-SKI
Length 2.50 m (8 ft) x beam 600 mm (2 ft)

(Metric measures)

Parts	Gelcoat kg	Lam. resin kg	CSM 445 gm/m² Metres²	No. of layers	Potch kg	Additional materials
Deck	0.8	3.5	3.5	2		
Hull	0.8	3.5	3.5	2		
Gunwale joint (laminated)		1	1	2		
Gunwale joint (potched)					1.5	
Joining seat insert					0.25	
Hull and deck re-inforcement		1	1	2		
						1 drain plug, rope and toggle, PU foam system

(Imperial measures)

Parts	Gelcoat lb	Lam. resin lb	CSM 445 gm/m² Feet²	No. of layers	Potch lb	Additional materials
Deck	2	7.5	36	2		
Hull	2	7.5	36	2		
Gunwale joint (laminated)		2	10	2		
Gunwale joint (potched)					3	
Joining seat insert					0.5	
Hull and deck re-inforcement		2	10	2		
						1 drain plug, rope and toggle, PU foam system

The buoyancy available to support the user is directly proportional to the sealed volume of the surf-ski. This should be kept in mind when hiring a mould or building a plug. A 2.50 m (8 ft) ski will support a paddler of up to 70 kg (156 lb) in weight, but a surf-ski of minimum length 3 m (10 ft) will be required by heavier persons.

Because the broad, flat bottom of the ski is very flexible, rigidity must be built in after the hull has been moulded. GRP core stringers are the most effective and easiest to install.

Construction

The same lay up techniques are followed as for the slalom canoe moulding, including the fitting of GRP reinforcement corrugations. In the case of the ski, three equally spaced corrugations should be laid up along the hull and possibly two in the deck moulding behind the seat. Polyurethane foam should be poured into the completed ski by means of a small hole, drilled just behind the seat position. This should be done after the nylon drain plug hole is cut out so that the gas given off by the expanding foam can escape. The foam gives extra rigidity to the ski around the seat area, with minimum weight gain. The small hole is plugged, with the appropriately coloured gelcoat, cut back and polished to give an invisible repair.

Joining the mouldings

The ski is laid up in two moulds — deck and hull. The deck mould is usually about 4 mm (⅛ in) wider than the hull mould, all round its top edge, so that the deck moulding overlaps the hull moulding at the gunwale joint.

There are two methods which can be used to bond the parts together. First, by cementing the joint on the inside, using a polyester filler, and second, by laminating over the joint on the inside, as for the slalom canoe.

Both these methods require further explanation as it would appear to be impossible to work on the inside of the join, because there is no cockpit opening.

Method 1 (a)   A small 'rim' mould is made up to match the gunwale edge of the deck moulding, but allowing enough clearance for a slot to be formed between the subsequent rim moulding and the edge of the deck. The rim moulding is laid up separately using only one layer of 445 gm/m² (1½ oz/ft²) CSM and no gelcoat. After cure, the rim moulding is trimmed, pulled from its mould and secured in place, level with the top edge of the deck moulding, using one layer of pre-soaked CSM, approximately 75 mm (3 in) wide.

After cure, the groove or slot so formed round the rim of the

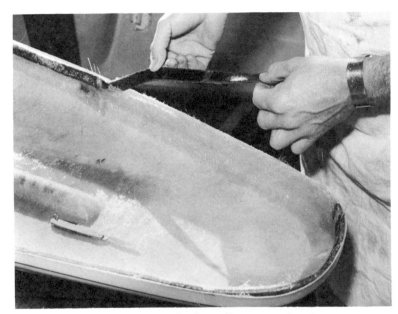

Rubber used to form a CSM rim is easily removed and can be used a number of times before it must be replaced.

An overlap on the deck mould allows the hull mould to be bonded inside it. The methods used are described in the text.

deck is filled with potch and the edge of the hull moulding is pressed into it. It is important that all PVA solution, mould release wax and gelcoat glaze are removed from the edge of the hull before it is inserted, otherwise the bond will be weak and will probably fracture during rigorous use. All excess potch is wiped from the join, before it gels, by means of a rag soaked in acetone. The exterior edge of the join is then finished off using one of the methods described for the slalom canoe.

Method 1 (b)   If a rim mould is not available, or the time and effort involved in making one cannot be justified, a much simpler alternative method can be used. The groove is formed using a strip of sponge rubber (approximate section 25 mm x 4 mm [1 in x

⅛ in] black door seal rubber) which is temporarily secured to the inside edge of the deck moulding using cellophane tape. One layer of 445 gm/m² (1½ oz/ft²) is pre-soaked, on the bench, and stippled gently against the rubber strip and a narrow area of the moulding underneath it. Once the lay up has gelled it is trimmed level with the top of the deck and the rubber is removed by pulling gently. The jointing procedure is then carried out exactly as described before.

Note: The rubber strip can be used repeatedly without any surface treatment such as PVA or wax, provided it is removed at the initial gel (or 'toffee') stage of the laminate. If the rubber is left in place until total cure is reached then it will have to be prized out using a knife and may become too badly torn to be re-used.

Method 2   In order to gain access to the interior of the ski so that the joint can be laminated inside in the conventional manner, a section of the deck is cut out. If the deck mould has been designed with this type of construction in mind the whole seat area, including heel indentations, will have been marked out, possibly by a non-skid pattern or a raised strip in the gelcoat. This makes for easy cutting as no measuring and marking is required.

The procedure is as follows:

1 After trimming and removal from the mould, the deck area around the seat and heel sockets is carefully removed by means of a power jig saw. The cut edges are then sanded down.
2 The two cut portions of the deck are replaced in the mould and masking tape is used to seal the joint and an area of approximately 20 mm (¾ in) round the edge of the seat portion.

The section of deck cut out to provide access to the interior of the ski in order to bond the joint between hull and deck mouldings. The deck moulding has been replaced in the mould for ease of working — the black area is the mould from which the cut out section has been lifted.

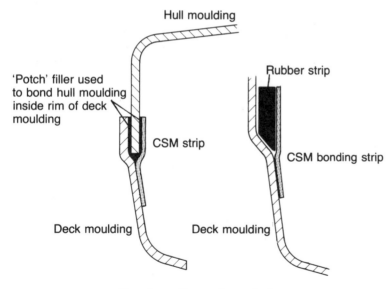

Showing rubber strip method.

56

3 80 mm (3 in) wide strips of 445 gm/m² (1½ oz/ft²) CSM are pre-soaked and bonded to the larger portion of the deck but at the same time allowing a 20 mm (¾ in) 'border' to rest on the masking tape. Three layers of CSM should be used in this operation and they should be stippled and rolled down carefully.

4 The laminate is trimmed to the inner edge of the masking tape at the 'toffee' stage and the mouldings are separated to reveal a 20 mm (¾ in) lip round the edge of the cut-out section. The edge of the lip, along with the lip surface, is sanded down with 100 grit garnet paper in preparation for joining later.

5 The deck and hull are now pressed together and sealed on the outside with masking tape.

6 The craft is now set up on edge and the joint laminated inside as described for the slalom canoe.

7 After cure, the seat area is cemented into position using a polyester filler. The small cut between the mouldings is filled and all excess potch is wiped from the surface of the deck with a rag soaked in acetone. Masking tapes can also help to avoid mess during this operation.

Both the gunwale edge and the seat insert joint can be masked off, surface prepared, and two layers of glassfibre tape applied to cover the joints. The glassfibre tape is cut back after cure and a coloured flow coat applied. The masking tape is then removed. Both of the joints can also be covered simply by applying a gelcoat stripe as described for the slalom canoe.

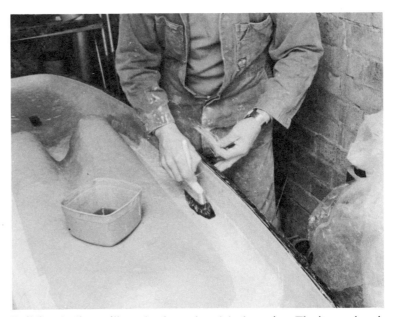

Building the lip or sill to take the replaced deck section. The inner piece is covered with tape while a CSM strip is bonded to the outer part of the moulding and overlaps onto the removable section.

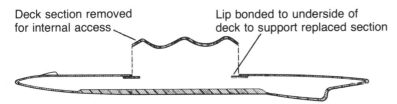

Cross section of a moulded surf-ski showing method of lifting deck section for internal access, and construction of GRP lips to support replaced deck section.

Notes: A nylon drain plug should be fitted at some convenient point on the deck of the surf-ski. A silicon sealing compound should be used when fitting the plug. Its purpose is to allow easy drainage and ventilation of the ski should the skin be punctured, and also to equalise internal/external pressures in hot conditions, particularly when the ski is not being used.

A lifting toggle should be attached to the bow of the ski in the interests of safety and convenience. Often, fitting the toggle simply entails drilling through a raised nodule in the deck. Alternatively, a rope is knotted through the deck and laminated in position to prevent leaks, *before* deck and hull mouldings are joined.

A coloured flow coat covers the join where the deck section was removed. Done correctly, it can enhance the appearance of the craft while at the same time covering the blemishes caused by removing the deck section.

BUILDING A SURF-YAK

Construction

The GRP lay-up, the reinforcing of deck and hull and the bonding of deck to hull are all identical to the procedures used in the slalom canoe construction. The seat and coaming are also fitted in the same manner but before doing so, buoyancy compartments should be built into the GRP shell. The surf-yak is designed for use in extremely rigorous conditions and so as much buoyancy as possible is sealed into the craft in the form of air compartments locked behind solid marine-ply or GRP bulkheads.

There are a number of reasons for using this system of buoyancy in the yak, as opposed to foam blocks or poured polyurethane foam. These are:

1 The bulkheads can be positioned so that the maximum air cavities are utilised. Usually one is located immediately behind the back edge of the cockpit and the other in a comfortable foot-rest position.

2 The bulkheads are relatively cheap and easy to make and fit.
3 They add extra structural strength to the GRP shell at two positions of high stress — halfway down the foredeck where the pressure can be enormous when the yak buries its nose in the surf, and just behind the cockpit where the canoeist rests his weight as he gets in and out of the craft.
4 They provide the lightest and cheapest form of buoyancy.
5 The forward bulkhead makes a secure and comfortable foot rest.

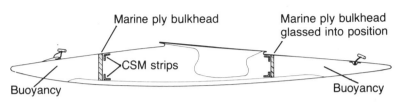

Section through surf yak showing buoyancy chambers.

MATERIALS REQUIRED TO MOULD A SURF-YAK
Length 3 m (10 ft) x beam 600 mm (2 ft)

(Metric measures)

Parts	Gelcoat kg	Lam. resin kg	CSM 445 gm/m² Metres²	No. of layers	Potch kg	Additional materials
Deck	1	4	4	2		
Hull	1	4	4	2		
Deck and coaming	0.25	1.5	1.5	Deck 4 Coaming 2		
Deck and hull reinforcement		1	1	2		
Deck and hull joining		1.5	1.5	2		
Bulkheads x 2		1.5	1.5	2		Marine ply x 9 mm thick
Coaming and deck joining					0.25	Rope and toggles, 2 drain plugs

(Imperial measures)

Parts	Gelcoat lb	Lam. resin lb	CSM 1½ oz/ft² Feet²	No. of layers	Potch lb	Additional materials
Deck	2	9	40	2		
Hull	2	9	40	2		
Deck and coaming	0.5	3.5	16	Deck 4 Coaming 2		
Deck and hull reinforcement		2	10	2		
Deck and hull joining		3.5	16	2		
Bulkheads x 2		3.5	16	2		Marine ply x ⅜ in thick
Coaming and deck joining					0.5	Rope and toggles, 2 drain plugs

Fitting the bulkheads

1 Sit in the canoe and get someone to mark your toe position on the deck with a pencil. (The foot can usually be detected as a shadow against the laminate.)
2 Use templates to mark out the appropriate shape of the bulkheads at their respective positions.
3 Shape the bulkheads using a bandsaw, jig saw or coping saw and fit them by means of a surform file, spokeshave or sanding disc.
4 Bulkheads should either be made of 9 mm (⅜ in) marine-ply bonded to the GRP shell with 2 layers of 445 gm/m² (1½ oz/ft²) CSM or some thinner section of marine-ply suitably reinforced with layers of GRP over the whole surface.
5 After cure, the laminate is sanded down to remove any sharp fibres and a flow coat is applied. The seat is then fitted as described previously.

Lifting toggles

These should be fitted to both ends of the surf-yak and like the surf-ski the yak frequently has nodules moulded into the deck which make for easy attachment of the toggles after assembly of the craft. Alternatively the toggles must be drilled through the deck laminate and glassed into position after removal from the mould but before the bulkheads are fitted. Unlike the ski, the yak toggles cannot be fitted before assembly of the shells as the yak is normally bonded while still in the moulds.

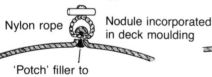
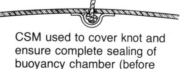

Wooden toggle

Nylon rope   Nodule incorporated in deck moulding

'Potch' filler to ensure complete sealing of buoyancy chamber

CSM used to cover knot and ensure complete sealing of buoyancy chamber (before joining deck to hull)

Fitting the lifting toggles.

The strongest and neatest method of finishing toggle rope is an eye splice.

1 Drill two holes through the deck, one near the bow and the other close to the stern.
2 Push a length of light wire through each hole in turn and retrieve the end from the cockpit. Thread the wire through one end of the lifting rope and tie a knot in the other.
3 Pull the wire and rope back up the inside of the yak and out the hole. Attach a toggle to the rope as in the slalom canoe. The procedure is repeated for the other toggle.
4 The yak is now inverted between two benches, and pre-soaked squares of CSM are used to cover and seal the knots on the inside of the deck.

The gunwale join is sealed on the outside by means of PVC tape, glassfibre tape, polyester filler and paint or gelcoat stripe — as described for previous craft.

BUILDING SMALL BOATS

1. rowing dinghy
2. fishing boat
3. sailing dinghy

MATERIALS REQUIRED TO MOULD A SMALL ROWING DINGHY
Length 2 m (6.5 ft) x beam 1.5 m (5 ft)

Complete with two built in buoyancy chambers which provide the seating.

(Metric measures)

Parts	Gelcoat kg	Lam. resin kg	CSM 445 gm/m² Metres²	No. of layers	Potch kg	Additional materials
Hull	2.5	8	8	2		SS painter ring, 1 pair SS rowlock plates
Seat mouldings cum buoyancy chambers	1	3	3	2		2 x 125 mm diam. plastic inspection hatches
Keel reinforcement		0.5	0.5	2	0.5	Timber keel strip inlay 2 Oregon pine blocks
Rowlock blocks and outboard motor pad		0.5	0.5	2		200 x 200 x 15 mm marine ply OM pad
Seat moulding reinforcements		1	1	2		PU foam, timber or cardboard core materials
Flow coat		0.5				Pigments, catalyst, etc.

(Imperial measures)

Parts	Gelcoat lb	Lam. resin lb	CSM 1½ oz/ft² Feet²	No. of layers	Potch lb	Additional materials
Hull	5.5	17.5	84	2		SS painter ring, 1 pair SS rowlock plates
Seat mouldings cum buoyancy chambers	2	6.5	32	2		2 x 5 in diam. plastic inspection hatches
Keel reinforcement		1	5	2	1	Timber keel strip inlay 2 Oregon pine blocks,
Rowlock blocks and outboard motor pad		1	5	2		8 x 8 x ½ marine ply OM pad
Seat moulding reinforcements		2	10	2		PU foam, timber or cardboard core materials
Flow coat		1				Pigments, catalyst, etc.

MATERIALS REQUIRED TO MOULD A FISHING BOAT
Length 5 m (17 ft) x beam 2 m (6.5 ft)

Complete with side decks, seating and buoyancy chambers, laminated as one unit, and bonded to the hull.

(Metric measures)

Parts	Gelcoat kg	Lam. resin kg	CSM 445 gm/m² Metres²	No. of layers	Potch kg	Additional materials
Hull (bottom and transom)	4	35	30	5		Outboard motor pad. Marine grade multi-ply 25 mm thick bolted to transom
Hull (sides)	3	22	20	4		
Side decks	2.5	18	16	4		
Seating/buoyancy chambers	3	17	15	3		
Reinforcement of seating areas, side deck, etc.		2	2	2		PU foam, timber or cardboard core material
Reinforcement of hull (if necessary)	Depends on hull mould configurations, re curves, chines, keel ridge, flutes, etc., designed into hull shape, may give sufficient rigidity.					
Bonding mouldings together		2	2	2	2	Deck/hull join, flanges etc.
Flow coat		2				Pigments, catalyst, etc.

(Imperial measures)

Parts	Gelcoat lb	Lam. resin lb	CSM 1½ oz/ft² Feet²	No. of layers	Potch lb	Additional materials
Hull (bottom and transom)	9	77	315	5		Outboard motor pad. Marine grade multi-ply 1 in thick, bolted to transom
Hull (sides)	6.5	48	210	4		
Side decks	5.5	40	168	4		
Seating/buoyancy chambers	6.5	37	158	3		
Reinforcement of seating areas, side decks, etc.		4.5	21	2		PU foam, timber or cardboard core material
Reinforcement of hull (if necessary)	Depends on hull mould configurations, re curves, chines, keel ridge, flutes, etc., designed into hull shape, may give sufficient rigidity.					
Bonding mouldings together		4.5	21	2	4.5	Deck/hull join, flanges etc.
Flow coat		4.5				Pigment, catalyst, etc.

MATERIALS REQUIRED TO MOULD A SAILING DINGHY
Length 3.5 m (11.5 ft) x beam 1.75 m (5.8 ft)

Complete with GRP side decks, seating and buoyancy chambers, laminated as one unit and bonded to the hull.

(Metric measures)

Parts	Gelcoat kg	Lam. resin kg	CSM 445 gm/m² Metres²	No. of layers	Potch kg	Additional materials
Hull including centreboard casing	4	17	15	3		SS painter ring, SS chainplates, SS rowlock plates, pintles
'Top' moulding incl. parts listed above	2.5	10	10	3		SS sailing fittings, cleats etc. drain plugs
Reinforcement of seating areas		1.5	1.5	2		PU foam, timber or cardboard core materials
Laminating of top moulding to hull at flanges		1	1	2		
'Cementing' of top moulding to hull (gunwale edge etc.)					1	
Flow coat		0.5				Pigments, catalyst, etc.

(Imperial measures)

Parts	Gelcoat lb	Lam. resin lb	CSM 1½ oz/ft² Feet²	No. of layers	Potch lb	Additional materials
Hull including centreboard casing	9	37	157	3		SS painter ring, SS chainplates, SS rowlock plates, pintles
'Top' moulding incl. parts listed above	5.5	21	105	3		SS sailing fittings, cleats etc. drain plugs
Reinforcement of seating areas	—	3.5	15	2		PU foam, timber or cardboard core materials
Laminating of top moulding to hull at flanges		2	10	2		
'Cementing' of top moulding to hull (gunwale edge etc.)					2	
Flow coat		1				Pigments, catalyst, etc.

The notes below apply to rowing dinghies, sailing dinghies and fishing boats up to approximately 5 m (say 16 ft) in length. Such craft are usually moulded in two or more parts which are then bonded together:

Part 1 The external or hull moulding, which in the case of a sailing dinghy, may incorporate a centreboard casing as an integral part of the hull lay-up.

Part 2 A matching internal or top moulding which may incorporate such parts as gunwale, decks, seats, buoyancy chambers, flooring.

In addition, this technique lends itself to such moulded inclusions as water-sheds, non-skid patterns, mast steps and outboard motor reinforcing. It is well worth the effort to incorporate these features in the plug, especially if a production run of mouldings is planned.

Construction

The GRP lay-up for small sailing and fishing boats is similar to that described for canoes except that any tight curves, such as

Non-skid and other patterns can easily be incorporated in the mould. A textured vinyl is used to achieve this non-skid seat.

those at the chines, transom and centreboard casing, should first be laminated using open weave glassfibre tape or 'split' strips of 445 gm/m^2 (1½ oz/ft^2) CSM, in order to 'bind' the gelcoat in these areas and prevent chipping during use. This initial lay-up is allowed to gel before the main lamination work is tackled.

Forming a centreboard casing

There are a number of methods used to construct a centreboard casing. It can be fabricated separately in timber or GRP and fitted into the hull moulding after cure. If the hull mould is in two halves, split along the keel, the join will run along the length of the centreboard casing. This allows the casing to be laid up in two halves along with the hull. The hull and centreboard casing are then joined after release from the split mould. The most common — and best — system is to mould the centreboard casing as an integral part of the hull moulding. A tapered plug of solid timber, or a wedged (collapsible) plug made of masonite, pineboard or plywood is constructed, the plug surface sealed as described previously and set up in the appropriate position in the hull mould. Plaster fillets, of minimum radius 6 mm (¼ in), are required at the join of centreboard and mould surface. The

Centreboard casing incorporated as part of a split mould.

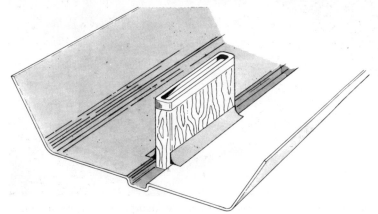

Timber centreboard casing screwed and laminated to the hull moulding.

plasterwork is sealed using shellac and the whole mould and plug carefully waxed and coated with PVA solution. After curing, the moulding is 'pulled' complete with plug still inside the centreboard lay-up. The plug is then removed either by driving it out against the taper or by removing wedges and collapsing the plug fabrication, leaving the centreboard casing as part of the hull moulding.

Bonding the parts together

Side deck and interior mouldings of a dinghy are normally bonded to the hull moulding while it is resting in the mould in order to avoid distortion and ensure a perfect match where the different mouldings come together. Bonding usually involves 'cementing' the parts together using a polyester filler but internal GRP fittings frequently incorporate small flanges which rest against the hull and are laminated to it by means of two layers of 445 gm/m^2 (1½ oz/ft^2) CSM.

The centreboard casing is moulded round a fabricated plug fitted into the mould. The plug can be made of a number of materials including timber or masonite and finished with plaster.

When bonding GRP mouldings by means of flanges two points should be kept in mind:

1 It is essential to remove PVA solution, mould release wax and the polished gelcoat finish from the flange before laminating, otherwise the laminating resin will not form a permanent bond with the flange and will separate during use. The gelcoat on the flange is cut back with 100 grit garnet paper to provide the necessary key for laminating.

Laying up the centreboard casing together with the rest of the hull moulding. Note the vertical timber secured to the ceiling to hold plug rigid during moulding operations.

2 Masking tape should be used on the flanged mouldings to avoid having to spend time cleaning brush marks and drips of resin from the finished work. The masking tape should be left in position until all loose fibres have been sanded down and a flow coat has been applied to the moulding.

Timber fittings

Before attaching timber fittings such as rowlock brackets, thwarts, outboard motor pad, and bulkheads, the moulding

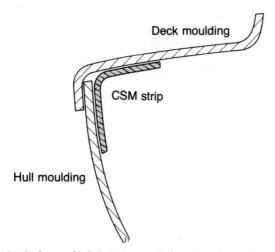

Deck moulding

CSM strip

Hull moulding

The most basic form of joining two mouldings in CSM strip laid up inside the join.

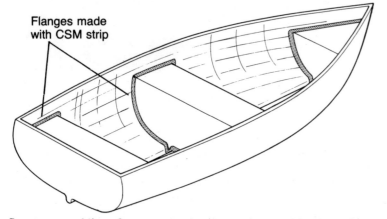

Flanges made with CSM strip

Separate mouldings for seats can be glassed into position with flanges made from CSM tape. These seats, if well sealed into position, double as buoyancy chambers.

should be allowed to cure for at least 24 hours. This will avoid 'print through' or distortion of the lay-up laminate and gelcoat. Timber fittings are usually potched or taped in place and then covered with laminations of GRP.

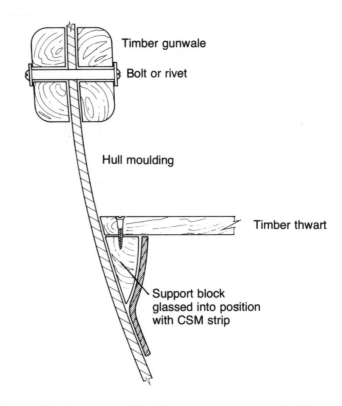

Timber gunwale

Bolt or rivet

Hull moulding

Timber thwart

Support block glassed into position with CSM strip

Methods used for securing wooden fittings such as gunwale and timber thwarts to GRP moulded hull.

Metal fittings
Metal fittings can be locked in position using GRP laminations as described for timber but in the majority of cases metal parts are screwed or bolted onto the GRP using thrust washers or pressure pads (either timber or metal) to help spread the load. A silicon or rubber sealing compound should always be used under metal fittings as it is important to prevent leaks through the laminate. Typical metal dinghy fittings include mooring cleats and tow rings, chainplates, jam cleats, self bailers and rudder pintles.

Metal keel strips
Most GRP dinghy hulls are fitted with metal keel strips to protect the gelcoat surface from abrasion. These strips are usually made of aluminium or brass strap, approximate section 25 mm (1 in) x 3 mm (⅛ in), and are secured to the GRP hull using small, stainless steel, self-tapping, countersunk screws.

Note: There is a slight electrolysis problem here caused by the dissimilar metals in contact, but if the boat is kept out of the water it should not be very great. If, however, the craft is to be kept permanently moored in salt water then this system should not be used. Instead, a stainless steel strap, using stainless steel self-tapping screws, would be more permanent, albeit more expensive.

5 BUILDING SURFBOARDS, SURF-SKIS AND SAILBOARDS

This technique makes use of male formers as opposed to the female mould used in previous craft. A male former of polyurethane foam (called a blank) is shaped to the required dimensions and profile of the board or ski, and the blank is then 'cocooned' in GRP. These blanks are 'foamed up' or cast in split moulds by the manufacturer and so conform roughly to the finished shape of the work, but are considerably larger all round to allow for hand forming to individual requirements.

Surfboard blanks can be purchased in a variety of sizes, and larger blanks, suitably moulded for use as wave-skis or sailboards are also available. Blanks are supplied as plain castings or, at additional cost, can be obtained with the central insert running down its length. Inserts or 'stringers' are commonly made from material such as a coloured polyester resin glue line, a soft timber veneer, usually red cedar, with a coloured resin glue line on each side, or a plywood veneer — usually used in the heavier wave-ski blanks.

The blank is split down its centre after moulding and rebonded with the stringer of required material and colouring inserted. This stringer performs three main functions in that it provides a decorative effect on the finished board or ski, it adds rigidity to the blank thus reducing 'drumming' or vibration during use, and it acts as a guide when shaping the top and bottom surfaces of the blank.

Forming the blank

1 Draw out the required board shape (full size) on a sheet of cardboard.
2 Cut out the shape, position it carefully on the blank and mark round it with a pencil or scriber.
3 Cut the blank to the marked shape using any suitable saw, such as a bandsaw, hacksaw, panel saw or keyhole saw.
4 Complete the rough shaping of edges and ends using a surform file or power planer.
5 Using 40 grit garnet paper wrapped round a cork pad, cut back the surface of the blank to its final thickness.

BUILDING A SURFBOARD

MATERIALS REQUIRED TO BUILD A SURFBOARD AND SURF-SKI USING FOAM BLANKS

(Metric measures)

	205 gm/m² cloth length in metres	Lam. resin kg	MEKP ml	Filler coat resin kg	MEKP ml	Finishing coat resin kg	MEKP ml
Surfboard							
Top lay-up	2	0.5	8	0.6	10	0.25	10
Bottom lay-up	2	0.5	8	0.6	10	0.25	10
Fin fittings	Cloth cuttings and rovings	0.2	3				
Kneeling pad	0.5						
Approx. totals	4.5	1.2	1.2			0.5	
Surf-ski	**330 gm/m² cloth**						
Deck	3	1.0	15	1.0	18	0.5	20
Deck reinforcement lay-up	1	0.25	4				
Hull	2 x 3	1.8	25	1.0	18	0.5	20
Fin fitting (Methods 1 & 2)	Cloth cuttings and rovings	0.2	3				
Approx. totals	10	3.25		2		1	

(Imperial measures)

	6 oz/yd² cloth length in yards	Lam. resin lb	MEKP ml	Filler coat resin lb	MEKP ml	Finishing coat resin lb	MEKP ml
Surfboard							
Top lay-up	2.2	1.1	8	1.3	10	0.6	10
Bottom lay-up	2.2	1.1	8	1.3	10	0.6	10
Fin fitting	Cloth cuttings and rovings	0.5	3				
Kneeling pad	0.5						
Approx. totals	5.0	2.7		2.6		1.2	
Surf-ski	**10 oz/yd² cloth**						
Deck	3.3	2.2	15	2.2	18	1.1	20
Deck reinforcement lay-up	1.1	0.6	4				
Hull	2 x 3.3	4	25	2.2	18	1.1	20
Fin fitting (Methods 1 & 2)	Cloth cuttings and rovings	0.5	3				
Approx. totals	11	7.3		4.4		2.2	

Note: The glassfibre cloth is purchased by the metre (yard) and is 675 mm (27 in) wide, so lengths only are given in the tables.

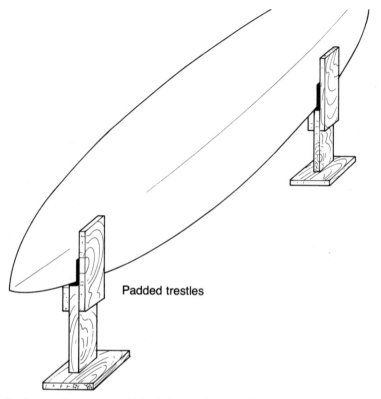

Padded trestles

Setting up the surfboard blank for cutting, shaping and working prior to glassing.

6 Smooth off all surfaces using a piece of brass fly-wire. Handle the blank with care from now on as the foam is easily dented.
7 Mark out the fin slot on the underside, to the following dimensions:

  Length — about 6 mm (¼ in) longer than the fin itself.
  Width — 15 mm (⅝ in).
  Depth — 12 mm (½ in).

Shaping the blank with a surform file. Note use of face mask and padded trestles.

The distance of the slot from the end of the board is a matter of personal preference.
8 Cut out the fin slot using a thin bladed trimming knife and chisel. The blank is now ready for the lay-up.
  Note: Wear a face mask when shaping and sanding the blank to avoid inhalation of dust.

Three types of resin are used for the board construction in this order:
1 A laminating resin for the laminating coat.
2 A filler resin for the filler coat.
3 A thin outer gelcoat for the finishing coat.

Laying up the lamination
1 Run a broad strip of masking tape round the underside of the blank, just to the inside of the curved edge.

2 Turn the board the right way up and place in position a kneeling pad of 204 gm/m² (6 oz/yd²) glass cloth of about 0.5 m² (½ yd²).

3 Drape a length of 204 gm/m² (6 oz/yd²) cloth over the blank and using scissors trim so that approximately 50 mm (2 in) of excess cloth hangs down from the edge of the blank, all round.

4 Carefully cut a 'V' slot in the cloth at the front of the board so that the material will 'lie' over the nose.

Note: Approximately 1.2 kg (2.7 lb) of laminating resin is required to 'cocoon' the blank and fit the fin. Fairly 'hot' mixes of resin are used in this type of construction, as the three successive coatings of resin are quickly applied.

5 An opaque pigment or translucent dye will be required to colour or tint the 1.2 kg (2.7 lb) of laminating resin.

The pre-cut cloth is laid on the blank and trimmed to shape.

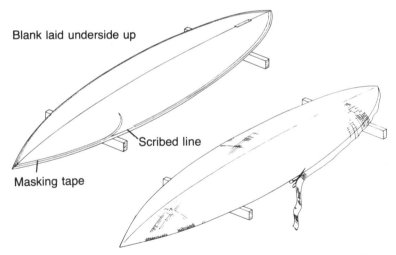

Blank laid underside up

Scribed line

Masking tape

'V' slot cut in cloth to accommodate sharp corner

Edge trimmed leaving sufficient overlap to reach masking tape

Laying and cutting the cloth on the shaped blank. After trimming the blank is turned over and the overlap taped down on the underside.

6 At a working temperature of, say, 21°C (70°F) add 8 ml (1/3 fl oz) of MEKP to 0.5 kg (1 lb) of tinted resin in a separate container.

7 Stir thoroughly, and carefully pour most of the resin along the cloth surface. Using a 'squeegee' spread the resin evenly over the whole surface.

8 Lift the edge overlaps on to the top of the blank and soak them thoroughly.

9 Using a brush, apply the remainder of the resin to the curved edge of the blank, as far as the masking tape, and then turn down the wet cloth and press it gently into position. All excess resin, and any air blisters under the cloth, must be removed with the squeegee.

10 After cure, invert the blank and cut off the flashing with a trimming knife, using the masking tape as a guide. The tape is also removed at this stage.

Pouring the resin. A squeegee is usually favoured over a brush on this job for obtaining a smooth, even application.

The whole procedure is now repeated on the other side of the blank and the fin slot trimmed out after cure. The masking tape is again used under the curved edge to provide a clean line when trimming off the excess cloth, and also to protect the previous lay-up from drips, runs, brush marks, finger marks, etc.

Fitting the fin

The surfboard fin can be constructed simply by laying up a thick GRP laminate on any suitable flat surface such as a sheet of glass, tinplate or Laminex. The lay-up consists of alternate layers of woven rovings and CSM built up to a thickness of approximately 6 mm (¼ in). After cure the laminate is cut to shape using a power jigsaw, bandsaw, or coping saw, and tapered down to the required finish by means of a power sander, surform file and garnet paper.

The finished shape is then cut back using silicon carbide (wet and dry paper) and polished to a high lustre using a burnishing

compound. Alternatively, the fin can be purchased as a shaped blank, ready for tapering and polishing, or as a finished item ready to insert in the fin slot.

1 Carefully cut 10 strips of 204 gm/m² (6 oz/yd²) cloth to the length of the fin slot, and about 75 mm (3 in) wide.
2 Wet out 8 of the strips on a flat surface, using tinted laminating resin, and place them in the fin slot.
3 Press the fin firmly into the slot, line it up carefully so that it is vertical and exactly parallel to the centreline of the board.
4 Secure the fin in place using masking tape, until the lay-up gels.
5 Using short lengths of continuous rovings, and tinted laminating resin, build up a fillet on each side of the fin.
6 Wet out the remaining two strips of 204 gm/m² (6 oz/yd²) cloth, place them over the rovings and carefully form the whole lay-up into a smooth fillet curve with brush or fingers.

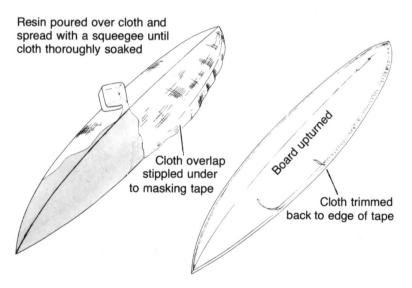

Resin poured over cloth and spread with a squeegee until cloth thoroughly soaked

Cloth overlap stippled under to masking tape

Board upturned

Cloth trimmed back to edge of tape

Showing the method of laying the laminate and trimming the underside.

Applying the filler coat

1 At a working temperature of, say, 21°C (70°F) add 10 ml (⅓ fl oz) MEKP to 0.6 kg (1 lb) of filler coat resin, and stir well in a separate container.
2 Apply the filler coat to the cured surface of the blank using a soft bristle brush. The underside, including the fin, is coated first.
3 Any drips which form under the edge must be carefully removed when the resin begins to gel.
4 Allow to cure, invert the blank and repeat the process on the top.

The 'hot' resin mix gives a limited pot life, and short initial gel time on the job (about 20 minutes). It is important, at this stage, to pay close attention to any ridges or lumps which, if not removed, will require filling and sanding when the cure is completed.

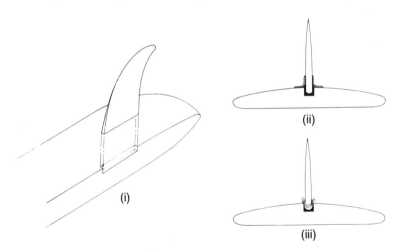

(i)

(ii)

(iii)

Three stages in fitting the fin. (i) The slot is cut to shape in the blank and the fin fabricated or purchased. (ii) Saturated strips of CSM are forced into the slot with the fin. (iii) Strips of CSM are used to secure the fin in place.

Masking tape is not used when applying the filler coat nor is dye or pigment paste added.

The filler coat is now sanded down to give a perfectly smooth surface, ready for application of the finishing coat. The sanding down must be done carefully so that the surface is not scored, especially at the edges. Power tools such as disc, belt or orbital sanders may be used carefully at this stage but the work can also be done by hand, using garnet paper on a cork pad. The grade of garnet paper used for the initial cut-back is 100 grit. This is then followed by a cut-back with 180 grit.

Note: A face mask, barrier cream and protective clothing should be used during this stage of the work.

Applying the finishing coat

1 Dry rub the board surface thoroughly to remove all dust.
2 Apply masking tape along the inside of the edge curve, on the underside, to catch drips and runs.
3 At a working temperature of, say, 21°C (70°F) add 10 ml (1/3 fl oz) MEKP to 0.25 kg (½ lb) of finishing coat resin and stir well in a separate container.
4 Apply the resin thinly and evenly to the top surface of the board using a soft bristle brush.
5 Allow it to gel and then remove the masking tape.
6 After cure the board is retaped, inverted and the procedure repeated on the underside.

The finishing coat resin contains wax in styrene, and is also a very 'hot' mix. As a result this coating polymerises quickly and gives a smooth, clear, hard finish to the board. If sufficient care and effort have been put into sanding down the filler coat, the finishing coat will give a perfect result, straight from the brush, requiring only to be polished and waxed prior to use.

BUILDING A SURF-SKI

The construction method is identical to that described in detail for building a surfboard. The work varies only in the quantity and weights of materials used, the shaping of the blanks and the fittings attached.

Shaping the blank

This is carried out as described for the surfboard, but in addition, seat and heel indentations are carved and sanded into the top surface of the ski. The seat hollow should be placed just behind the centre of gravity of the blank and the heel placings a suitable distance forward. The easiest and most accurate method of determining these positions is for the user to sit on the blank, in a comfortable paddling pose, and then mark round the three required points of contact.

Fitting the fin

There are three methods of fitting a fin to this type of surf-ski:

1 The method previously described for the surfboard.
2 A moulded plastic fin which is fitted with a flange and is screwed to the underside of the ski after construction using stainless steel self-tapping screws. This method simply requires a hollow, approximately 4 mm (3/16 in) deep, to be formed in the blank, under the area of the fin. The hollow is filled with strips of glassfibre cloth, CSM or a 'dough' mix to act as a reinforcement for the screw positions. The filled area is made 'flush' with the surface of the blank by pressing a strip of polythene or Laminex sheet over it and allowing to gel.
3 A plastic fin and matching fin box, which is fitted as a unit after construction of the ski. This system allows the fin to be removed, or its angle adjusted, for varying wave patterns and conditions.

A slot is cut in the blank to accommodate the fin box, with a few millimetres clearance all round. The top edges of the slot are given a 6 mm (¼ in) radius curve. Strips of glassfibre cloth are pre-soaked with laminating resin and used to line the slot.

The cloth is cut at the four top corners so that it can lie over the curved edges. After cure of the slot lining the cloth lay-up of the underside of the blank is proceeded with, as with the surfboard. Cuts are made in the cloth above the fin slot so that the material can be made to lie over the curved edges. After cure of the laminate the fin box is secured in place using a polyester filler.

Toe straps

There are three main types of toe fittings:
1 Nylon hinge plates containing flexible plastic toe straps which can be purchased complete.
2 Nylon rope loops running inside soft polyethelene tubing to give a comfortable grip.
3 50 mm (2 in) nylon seat belt webbing.

All types of fittings are screwed through the deck of the ski into previously reinforced areas of the foam blank. Such areas are hollowed out of the blank during shaping, and filled as described for the fin fitting in method 2. Stainless steel self-tapping screws and cup washers or pressure plates are used to secure the toe straps in place.

Different types of toe straps and usual method of securing them. From left — hinged plastic plate (complete unit), webbing strap, polythene tube containing nylon rope.

The lay-up

It follows that surf-ski laminations are heavier than those required for a board. Two layers of 330 gm/m² (10 oz/yd²) glassfibre cloth are used on the hull with either one or two layers of the same material applied to the deck, allowing a generous overlap at the edges of the ski. If only one layer of cloth is used on the deck, reinforcement layers of the same material should first be wetted out over the seat and heel positions.

The lay-up procedure is the same as for the surfboard except that in addition to the squeegee a brush is used to wet out the concave surfaces. Short-radius or 'star' shaped cuts are made in the cloth at the heel positions to allow the material to lie against the surface of the blank. Reinforcement strips previously applied should lie under the scissor cuts.

Material covering shallow seat indentations may not have to be cut as the cloth can be 'stretched' or 'formed' slightly after wet-out. If, however, cuts have to be made in the cloth to allow it to lie over the seat shape, once again, reinforcement strips of cloth must 'underlie' the slits in the lay-up material. All other aspects of the work are identical to the procedures listed for the surfboard.

BUILDING A SAILBOARD

MATERIALS REQUIRED TO MOULD A SAILBOARD
Length 4 m (12 ft 6 in) x beam 600 mm (2 ft)

(Metric measures)

Part	330 gm/m² cloth length in metres	Lam. resin kg	MEKP ml	Filler coat resin kg	MEKP ml	Finish- ing coat resin kg	MEKP ml
Sailboard							
Deck	2 x 4 m	2.5	30	1.25	24	0.75	25
Deck reinforcement lay-up	2	0.5	8				
Hull	2 x 4 m	2.5	30	1.25	24	0.75	25
Centreboard casing	Cloth cuttings	0.2	3				
Approx. totals	18	5.7		2.5		1.5	

Note: Glassfibre cloth can be purchased by the metre (yard) in a width of 675 mm (27 in) especially available for use with a foam blank approx. 600 mm (2 ft) wide — so lengths only are given.

There are a number of methods of building a sailboard, most of which are beyond the capacity of the amateur builder since they require sophisticated equipment or techniques. However, it is possible to construct a perfectly adequate sailboard by using the methods described for surfboards and surf-skis. The principle difference lies in the extra strength required to withstand the pressures of wind in the sails, and the fitting of slots for the centreboard and mast step.

(Imperial measures)

Part	10 oz/yd² cloth length in yards	Lam. resin lb	MEKP ml	Filler coat resin lb	MEKP ml	Finishing coat resin lb	MEKP ml
Sailboard Deck	2 x 4.3	6	30	3	24	1.5	25
Deck reinforcement lay-up	2	1	8				
Hull	2 x 4.3	6	30	3	24	1.5	25
Centreboard casing	Cloth cuttings	0.5	3				
Approx. totals	19.2	13.5		6		3	

Fitting the centreboard slot

The size of the centreboard slot will be determined by the size of the dagger and it is therefore necessary to obtain the rig before commencing construction of the board. With the cross section dimensions of the dagger board, mark out the inside measurements of the slot on the blank in rectangular form then mark a second rectangle, about 13 mm (½ in) outside the first. This allows for the slot casing to be fitted. The location of the slot should be approximately midway along the length of the board from the bow and just behind the location of the mast step. Cut out the outer rectangle with care, using a keyhole or jig saw, and sand back to a smooth finish.

The principal difference in building a sailboard is that it requires greater strength than a surfboard. Extra stringers in the blank and extra layers of laminate take care of this.

Now a box framework or casing must be made from 13 mm (½ in) marine grade plywood to fit the slot exactly. This should be well glued and screwed with stainless steel screws, and flushed to fit at the top and bottom of the board before the laminating coat is laid onto the blank. It should then be glassed into position using 330 gm/m² (10 oz/yd²) cloth just before the laminating lay-up commences so that the overlay of laminate on the top and bottom of the slot meets and creates a totally waterproof bond between centreboard casing and the main body of the board. To hold the dagger board firmly in position, it will be necessary either to shape the top of the dagger rectangular to fit the shape of the slot, or build-up the slot to match the shape of the dagger, which is usually streamlined.

Fitting the mast step

A similar casing is made for the mast step, which is fitted on the centreline, just ahead of the slot. In this case, however, the casing is only recessed to the required depth into the board, and not cut right through. The bonding procedure is the same as for the centreboard slot.

The lay-up

The additional strength required by the sailboard can be gained either by purchasing a blank that has been specially reinforced or by adding extra layers of cloth in the laminating lay-up process. Instead of the two layers of 330 gm/m² (10 oz/yd²) cloth used for the surf-ski, an additional layer should be applied. A strip of reinforcing cloth about 13 mm (½ in) wide laid along the centreline of the board will also add longitudinal strength and distribute the stresses in the vicinity of the mast step throughout the length of the board.

As mentioned earlier, the procedures for lay-up, filler and finishing coats are the same for a sailboard as for a surfboard or surf-ski. Some personal preferences may be applied to the shaping of the blank and some more expert 'windsurfers' may like to adjust the location of the centreboard (and thus the rig) to suit their individual styles. But beyond this and the extra weight of laminate for added strength, all lay-up procedures are similar to those described earlier.

6 PLUGS AND MOULDS

DESIGNING A PLUG

The design of the plug should capitalise, as far as possible, on the advantages of GRP as a mould making and moulding material, and should seek to minimise its shortcomings. It is important to be familiar with these 'plus' and 'minus' points, as GRP, like all other building materials, has its limitations. These must be kept in mind or errors will be made, and much time and effort will be needlessly expended.

The following is a list of good features and limitations associated with GRP as a building material.

Advantages

1 GRP materials are straightforward to activate and use by hand.
2 The gelcoat can be applied thick enough to allow cutting-back of the mould surface with wet or dry paper to remove surface blemishes left on the plug and imprinted onto the mould.
3 The laminate can be laid up on curved surfaces without difficulty — in fact curves help give the mould or moulding rigidity and should be incorporated in the plug construction where possible.
4 Rigidity can be designed into a plug, and the subsequent moulding, in the form of longitudinal surface 'Vs', corners, flutes and ridges.
5 On boat building these features will be present in the form of chine angles, gunwale flares, flanges and keels to maintain hull shape and minimise 'drumming' or flexing under load.

Limitations

1 The pot life (working time) is limited, so accuracy is required and care must be taken with brushes and rollers.
2 Radius curves of 6 mm (¼ in) are the minimum for normal CSM lay-up. Both concave and convex curves smaller than 6 mm (¼ in) should be 'designed out' of the plug.

So versatile is GRP that moulds can be made to produce almost any product. The secret behind both a good plug and a good mould is to avoid sharp angles and aim for good 'draw'.

3 GRP laminate is immensely strong and resilient for its weight but is susceptible to flexing and vibration. For this reason large flat areas on the plug should be avoided.
4 A mould should be left on the plug to cure for as long as possible up to a maximum of 4 weeks. This is seldom practicable but at least one week curing is essential or the mould will tend to warp during the latter cure period.
5 To prevent warping, flexing or drumming of the mould during its working life some form of bracing or stiffening is necessary. In small moulds this may simply mean potching the mould to a rigid base-plate or suitable brackets. In larger moulds some form of corrugation is usually attached to the outside to give rigidity where required.

Note. This type of reinforcement should always be secured to the mould while it is on the plug after initial cure has taken place (at least 24 hours after lay-up).

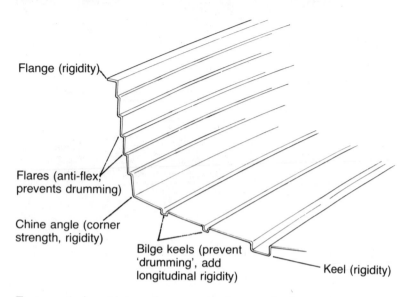

Flange (rigidity)

Flares (anti-flex, prevents drumming)

Chine angle (corner strength, rigidity)

Bilge keels (prevent 'drumming', add longitudinal rigidity)

Keel (rigidity)

Features designed into a plug — and subsequently the mould — to add strength and rigidity to the moulding.

6 Shrinking of the resin during cure is appreciable in laminating resin but cracking does not occur because of the binding effect of the glassfibre reinforcement. The resin will, however, cause shrinkage of the laminate on curves and especially in small radius corners. In fact, the smaller or tighter the corner the greater will be the pull on the resin. To avoid this problem, ensure that total cure has been effected prior to removal of the mould from the plug. A 'green' mould will pull in or distort alarmingly if removed from its plug too soon.

Constructing a plug

Materials that may be used for building a plug are many and varied. So also are the construction techniques employed to form the required plug shape. Sketches, scale drawings and working drawings of the construction procedure should be made and suitable materials for the work decided upon and procured. A suitable working area is necessary, bearing in mind that in some instances the plug structure may be very flimsy, perhaps with a limited working life. It may be impossible to move it around prior to the mould lay-up, without risk of damage.

For this reason, it should be constructed on a secure foundation in the moulding workshop, at a convenient working height. A base-plate such as a table, a work top supported on trestles, or a flat floor area will usually suffice as the starting point and polythene sheeting should be secured to it to minimise the mess caused during the mould lay-up.

Small plugs can often be constructed by shaping a solid piece of timber, plasticine, plaster or clay, applying a suitable surface finish and then moulding over the object with GRP. The plug is then 'pulled' from inside the mould or simply broken up to effect a release.

With larger work a basic framework of the required plug shape is secured to the base-plate and the contour shape of the product is built up on the frame, using the most suitable materials available. Normally some form of cladding or packing is secured to the framework and final filling and shaping is done using such materials as cement, plaster of Paris, cellulose plasters or polyester fillers. A few of the most common methods of constructing a plug are:

1. *Lath and plaster method*   A timber framework onto which is secured closely spaced, light timber laths acts as the base form and shape for a plaster screed coating. After sanding and filling, the screed coating is then sealed with a cellulose plaster, which in turn is sanded back until a plug surface, suitable for moulding on is produced. Shellac varnish is the best coating for the finished surface.

2 *Rigid cladding method*   A timber framework onto which are secured checked battens, forms the profile of the plug. A suitable rigid cladding such as plywood, masonite or Laminex is then cut, glued and pinned to the battens. All joints in the cladding,

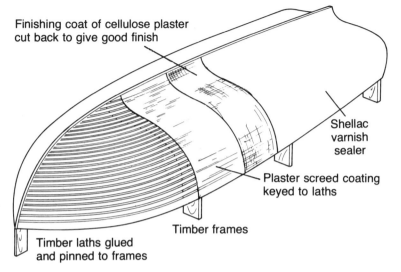

Finishing coat of cellulose plaster
cut back to give good finish

Shellac
varnish
sealer

Plaster screed coating
keyed to laths

Timber frames

Timber laths glued
and pinned to frames

Construction of a lath and plaster plug.

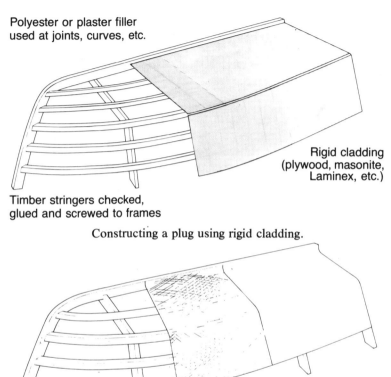

Polyester or plaster filler
used at joints, curves, etc.

Rigid cladding
(plywood, masonite,
Laminex, etc.)

Timber stringers checked,
glued and screwed to frames

Constructing a plug using rigid cladding.

Plaster coating
with shellac finish

Wire mesh

Interior of plug packed with
waste paper (not shown)

Constructing a plug using wire mesh and paper packing.

corners, fillets, nail and screw heads, etc., are then filled with cellulose plaster or polyester filler. The surface is sanded down and treated with resin flow coat.

3 *Packing and mesh wire method*   The timber and batten framework mentioned in method 2 forms the profile of the plug. The plug shape is then formed with waste paper and 12 mm (½ in) mesh wire is stretched over the stringers and stapled to them. The plug is then plastered as in method 1.

All of the above plugs are designed with the intention of laying up and 'pulling' a female GRP mould from them so that identical mouldings can be produced. A moulding can, however, be laid up directly onto a plug, thus dispensing with the female mould. This means, of course, that the moulding so formed will have a rough outside surface of GRP laminate rather than the smooth finish obtained in a female mould.

However, this can be quite acceptable where the smooth gelcoat is required on the inside. Typical examples of this type of mould are a swimming pool, a battery tray or an ice-box. In those cases the respective features most required are an effective water barrier, resistance to acid attack and an impervious, easily cleaned surface. All these features require a smooth internal gelcoat which can be laid up directly on the surface of the plug, with the exterior left rough.

Using the plug as a male mould is also practised where cutting back and flow coating the laminate surface after moulding gives an acceptable finish. This method is occasionally used in GRP boat hull construction. Some large yachts are laid up on a lath and plaster plug direct, and the plug dismantled on completion. With the use of sanding machines, fillers, flow coats and spray paints a perfect outer surface finish is achieved.

A plug used in this way need not have 'draw' designed into it as it can be dismantled or broken out of the moulding. This can be an advantage if a complex shaped moulding is required.

Drape moulding

This is a different technique in which application of the resin to the glassfibre cloth is done away from the work, and the soaked material is 'draped' over a special plug. A hessian cladding plug is mostly used as it is relatively quick to make and the moulding surface is not critical. The timber framework, including all stringers, should be coated with flow coat. After cure the framework is treated with mould release wax and PVA. Alternatively, all woodwork can be covered with masking tape. The hessian is then stapled over the frame and pulled as tight as possible.

Half the proposed GRP lay-up is draped over the hessian after first soaking the glassfibre material on a polythene covered bench. The glassfibre must be well soaked with resin as stippling and rolling of the laminate will cause sagging and stretching of the hessian and cannot therefore be used. The lay-up is allowed to cure and then the framework is broken out of the moulding along with any loose pieces of hessian. The majority of the hessian layer is left adhering to the laminate and the balance of the lay-up of GRP reinforcement is now applied to the inside of the moulding. Sanding down, filling and flow coating both inside and out will give an acceptable finish.

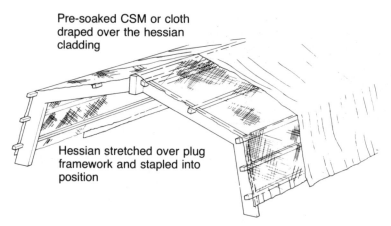

Pre-soaked CSM or cloth draped over the hessian cladding

Hessian stretched over plug framework and stapled into position

Drape moulding. It is important to ensure that the timber frame work is treated with flow coat resin and mould release wax as well as PVA before the hessian is applied. Failing this, the moulding may stick to the framework.

Glassfibre planking

This method of constructing a plug or moulding is really an extension of the draping method. Instead of hessian, a proprietary GRP sheeting material (usually called C-FLEX) is used. This can be purchased in coils approximately 30 m (100 ft) long by 300 mm (12 in) wide. The 'planking' consists of thin solid rods of GRP alternating with bundles of dry (un-resined) continuous glassfibre rovings. These run the whole length of the 'plank' and are held together by two layers of lightweight open weave glassfibre cloth, stitched dry to the rovings. This material is marketed in two weights — approximately 1.1 kg/m² (2lb/yd²) and 1.85 kg/m² (3½ lb/yd²). It is expensive but eliminates the need for an elaborate plug construction plus GRP female mould. For 'one-off' boat hulls, etc., it is a reasonably economical method of construction.

A timber frame is required as with the drape moulding technique and it also must be treated with a mould release agent or masking tape. The glassfibre planking is then cut to shape and stapled to the framework. Joints are butted, not overlapped, because of the thickness of the material. The planking is then coated with laminating resin to wet it out and layers of CSM are bonded to it in the normal manner. After cure the moulding is inverted, the framework removed and the balance of the lay-up applied to the interior. For finishing use the same procedures as for the hessian plug method.

MAKING A FEMALE MOULD

There are two sources from which a female mould can be made — an original product and a plug. Using an original product and producing copies of it may involve copyright problems, but provided these have been sorted out, taking a mould off an existing product can be a cheap and efficient way of obtaining good copies. A typical example would be the replacement of an old boat hull with a new GRP hull. If there is no copyright involved, or you have cleared the project with the designer, it is a relatively simple process to tidy up the old boat, take a mould off it, and produce a number of new GRP hulls off that mould, provided there are no 'return angles' which will prevent the mould from being lifted off the original hull.

The secret in obtaining a good mould lies in 'tidying up' the original product. Scratches and other indentations must be filled and smoothed flush with the surface, and any other imperfections put to rights, for every mark will be reproduced (and seemingly exaggerated) in the mould. This need not be an expensive process for fillers and shaping material such as plasticine or plaster can be used, rather than repairing the product with original material. The surface must be clean and dry with old paint removed. Flow coat brushed over the surface and then rubbed back and recoated will give the required finish, and from that point on it becomes a normal plug, and the procedure for taking off a mould is as follows:

Once the plug has been accurately shaped and given a smooth surface finish it can be treated with mould release wax and PVA

If the original product is in good condition and the surface is properly prepared, it is relatively easy to take a mould from it and produce subsequent replicas. Watch for copyright problems when using this method.

in readiness for the lay-up of the GRP mould. The mould construction involves the same steps as those described previously for the basic GRP lay-up technique, although a few additional factors relating specifically to a mould structure must be taken into consideration. These include:

The gelcoat.

The strength of the laminate.

Construction of flanges.

Framing, rigidity and suitable working base.

The gelcoat

In mould making the gelcoat should, for preference, be applied using tooling gelcoat which is especially formulated for this purpose. All gelcoat preparations will, of course, give reasonable results and for small moulds and mouldings the normal gelcoat preparation will suffice. In the case of larger moulds, however, it is worth the extra expense of using tooling gelcoat, especially if a high gloss professional finish is desired or if a large number of mouldings (say more than 20) are to be pulled from the mould. Here the resilience and durability of the tooling gelcoat will pay dividends. If the gelcoat is applied by brush, one coat of tooling gelcoat will suffice, but if a lambswool roller is used a second application should be added within an hour of gelation of the first coating.

After initial gelcoat cure the CSM laminations can be laid up, but before doing so it is worth considering the following points as they could improve the working life of the mould:

1 If the gelcoat surface of the mould is to be thoroughly cut back before polishing, and it is planned to pull a large number of mouldings from the mould, it is worth applying a thin coating of coloured gelcoat to the tooling gelcoat surface, by roller. This coloured gelcoat layer acts as a visual warning sign during the initial cutting back of the black tooling gelcoat, and also during future burnishing and repair work.

2 A layer of glassfibre surfacing tissue can be applied to the gelcoat surface prior to the CSM lay-up, helping to bind the gelcoat layer. This is a useful procedure if the gelcoat is applied to tight corners and small radius curves, and if the finished mould is going to be subjected to much flexing when mouldings are pulled from it.

3 The tight corners and curves mentioned above can be given further attention before the major lay-up work commences by again binding the gelcoat in these areas — this time using open weave glassfibre tape, continuous filament rovings or strips of 445 gm/m² (1½ oz/ft²) CSM split into half thicknesses simply by pulling gently. These precautionary measures can, on occasion, save many hours of frustrating gelcoat repair work once the mould is in use.

Tight angular changes of direction should be avoided at the design stage but occasionally they form an essential feature of the required shape, or perhaps cannot be eradicated from the male plug. In these instances the above procedure will help overcome the problems of gelcoat chipping or delamination. This reinforcement treatment should be allowed to complete its initial cure before the major lay-up is commenced.

The strength of the laminate

The laminate must be thick enough to give rigid support to the working surface of the mould, i.e. the gelcoat layer. Chopped strand mat is normally used for laminating and the number of layers required depends on the size and shape of the mould. As a rough guide a canoe or dinghy mould would require a minimum of three layers of 445 gm/m² (1½ oz/ft²) CSM as an overall basic reinforcement. As in all GRP hand lay-up work the mat is always overlapped at the joins — never butted. If these overlaps are thoughtfully planned so that they occur at regular spacings along the plug the resulting mould will have a series of double thickness 'ribs' built in and strategically placed.

Note: Six to eight layers of 445 gm/m² (1½ oz/ft²) CSM generates a considerable heat build-up during exotherm and so if a lay-up calls for laminations with an excess of four layers of

445 gm/m² (1½ oz/ft²) CSM (four overlaps make eight layers) then the lay-up should be carried out in two stages. This allows time for heat dissipation and reduces the risk of distortion and break-down of the resin.

Construction of flanges

Flanges are useful additions to a mould as they help prevent the mould edge from being damaged during trimming of the moulding, and also considerably improve the rigidity of the mould, thus helping it to keep its shape during use. Flanges can also be used as a means of securing split or matched moulds in perfect alignment using bolts, clamps or dowel pegs as in the case of the deck and hull moulds of a slalom canoe.

There are a number of methods for constructing flanges. Usually flanges form an integral part of the plug construction but they can also be built up on the mould laminate after lay-up. The easiest type of flange to make is the one formed between the base-plate and the inverted plug construction as in the case of a dinghy or slalom canoe gunwale.

In this case the base-plate should be treated with flow coat resin, mould release wax and PVA. Polythene sheeting should not be used to cover the base-plate unless a very heavy grade can be procured, as normal grades will wrinkle during polymerisation of the gelcoat. Because a relatively sharp edge is required at the top edge of a mould, plaster fillets should not be used between the plug and the base-plate. Instead, the gelcoat should be reinforced using continuous filament rovings or open weave glassfibre tape, before the main CSM lay-up is commenced.

If the type of flange described above does not touch the base-plate all round as, say, in the case of the curved gunwale edge of an eskimo kayak, paper packing and plaster must be used to build up a flange which will follow the contours of the plug edge. As an alternative to plaster and packing, paper templates can be made of the plug edge and masonite flange strips cut and fitted in position. Tinplate or zinc anneal flange strips can also be easily scribed and cut to shape using tinsnips.

If split moulds are to be taken from the plug the flange position is marked and flange strips are cut and fitted so that one half of

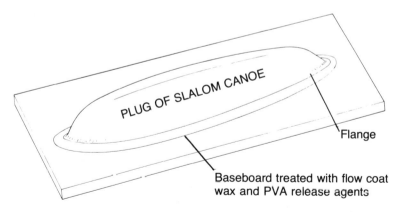

Construction of canoe plug on baseboard showing method of obtaining flange.

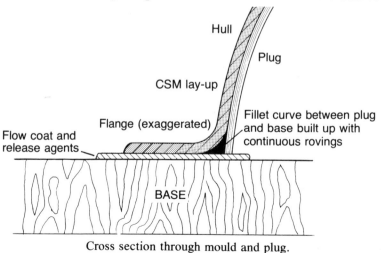

Cross section through mould and plug.

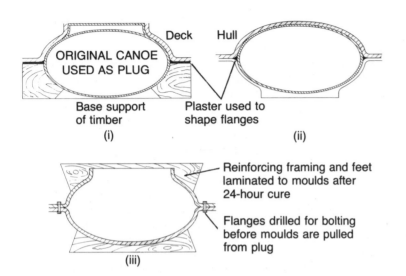

ORIGINAL CANOE USED AS PLUG

Deck   Hull

Base support of timber

Plaster used to shape flanges

(i)   (ii)

Reinforcing framing and feet laminated to moulds after 24-hour cure

Flanges drilled for bolting before moulds are pulled from plug

(iii)

Three steps in taking a split mould from an original product. (i) Deck and cockpit moulding laid up using timber framework and plaster to shape curve of flange. (ii) Hull mould laid up again using plaster for fillet curve. (iii) Finished split moulds reinforced by timber framing and ready for moulding.

the mould can be laid up. After cure the flange strips are removed, the exposed GRP flange treated, and the balance of the mould laid up. In this way a perfect match can be achieved between the two flanges. If bolting or dowelling is to be the method of joining the moulds the holes should be drilled through the flanges before the moulds are pulled from the plug.

Framing, rigidity and a suitable working base

The following points must be considered when building a mould:

1 The mould lay-up itself must be rigid enough to withstand the stippling and rolling action of moulding without vibrating.
2 The mould structure must be resilient enough to allow slight flexing to aid release of the moulding.

To avoid flexing or distortion the mould surfaces must be reinforced and supported. The flatter the mould surface, the more rigidity required.

3 The mould must be fitted with legs *or* placed in a cradle *or* secured to a firm base-plate *or* stand so that laminating and trimming a moulding in the mould is made easy.

If the GRP laminate itself does not give the mould sufficient rigidity then reinforcement can be laminated to the exterior of the structure after approximately 24 hours' cure time has elapsed. Reinforcement of the mould can take many forms. A few of the most common are:

1 Timber or chipboard frames bonded to the mould with GRP.
2 Corrugations of GRP laid over any pliable material which can be made to follow the mould contour. Rope, plastic hose, polyurethane foam strips and timber beading are typical materials for this work.
3 A welded steel frame or strips of angle iron, suitably potched and laminated to the mould structure.

7 TROUBLE SHOOTING

Sooner or later even the most careful GRP moulder will experience a few problems with the materials and complex chemicals being used. Problems can occur as a result of accidents, mistakes and unknown changes in working conditions.

Defects in hand lay-up GRP projects can usually be divided into two categories — gelcoat defects and defects in the reinforcement laminate. The table below lists some of the more common faults:

Gelcoat Defects

	Possible Cause	Action
PROBLEM 1: Gelcoat surface appears dull in places when 'pulled'	Rough mould surface. Wax build-up.	Cut back and rewax mould. Wash mould with warm water and soap solution. Dry and polish mould surface thoroughly with a large pad of cheesecloth.
	Polystyrene build-up.	If the build-up is heavy remove with the fingernail or the edge of a coin. If just beginning to show as a dull area on the mould, polish out with Brasso or similar burnishing compound. Rewax mould.
	Rough PVA coating.	Apply PVA solution evenly and gently with a clean piece of sponge or foam rubber.
PROBLEM 2: Fibre texture visible on surface of gelcoat.	Texture transferred from the surface of the mould.	Aged mould — may have to be replaced. But first try a hand cut-back, fill and repolish of the mould surface.
	Gelcoat application very thin or non-existent in places.	None, other than coat of polyurethane paint.
PROBLEM 3: Pattern of rovings or cloth apparent in the gelcoat ('print through').	Rovings or cloth laid up directly against gelcoat.	Never use these materials next to the gelcoat. 'Insulate' with CSM.
	Insufficient gelcoat. Low working temperature. Incorrect catalyst quantities.	No cure other than painting with coat of polyurethane.
	High exotherm of laminate causing excessive shrinking of the resin.	Watch mixing quantities and temperature chart.

	Possible Cause	Action
PROBLEM 4: Dull or soft spots in the gelcoat surface.	Uneven application of gelcoat.	Apply gelcoat more evenly by brushing gently in one direction only. If a roller is used apply gelcoat in two layers — allowing the first layer to polymerise before applying the second.
	Poorly mixed catalyst. Water or solvent on brush or roller.	Stir catalyst more thoroughly into the resin. Ensure that brush and roller are completely dry before use. Particularly check for water/solvent inside the metal brush frame and the roller tube.
PROBLEM 5: Porosity.	Trapped air.	Too vigorous mixing when adding catalyst and pigment to the resin.
	Excess catalyst.	Follow catalyst/resin weight/room temperature guide carefully.
PROBLEM 6: Pre-release — causing distortion in the form of cracking or blistering of the gelcoat prior to the laminate lay-up.	Catalyst quantity too high. Too long a gelcoat cure time prior to laminate lay-up, allowing the gelcoat to become brittle and more susceptible to mechanical damage.	Follow catalyst/temperature chart. Laminate should be applied as soon as possible after the initial cure of the gelcoat.
	Gelcoat applied too thickly or unevenly.	Apply evenly to obtain correct thickness with gentle brush sweeps or by roller.
	'Hot spots' or uneven cure.	Avoid this by mixing catalyst thoroughly and ensuring that the mould is kept at an even temperature (i.e. no draughts).
	Trapped solvent.	Check for water or acetone in mixing container, brush, roller, etc.
	Wet or excessive mould release coating (PVA).	Apply carefully and allow time for PVA solution to dry (especially in corners) before gelcoat application.
PROBLEM 7: Gelcoat cracks **(a):** Radial or 'spider' cracks.	Impact on the laminate surface of the moulding.	Avoid hammering the moulding while pulling from the mould.

	Possible Cause	Action
(b): Cracks forming concentric circles.	Impact on the gelcoat surface of the moulding.	Avoid accidental damage while the moulding is in use, or rough handling of the shell after 'pulling'.
(c): Long straight cracks either singly or in parallel lines.	Pre-release causing distortion. Excessive gelcoat thickness. Stress due to flexing.	See pre-release. See pre-release. Greater care in pulling of moulding. More care in handling of shell.
	Stress due to sticking in the mould.	Prepare mould thoroughly.
PROBLEM 8: Gelcoat wrinkling (also called 'alligatoring', 'triping', 'crow's feet'.)	Gelcoat insufficiently cured prior to lay-up of laminate. Gelcoat too thin.	Ensure that initial cure has occurred in the *lowest* part of the mould. Check gelcoat quantities and method of application. Also check the following: Gelcoat catalyst level. Working temperature. Length of gel time on the mould. Moisture or contamination (i.e. wax) on the mould surface.
PROBLEM 9: Poor bond between gelcoat and laminate.	Contamination.	Ensure that gelcoat surface is clean and 'tacky' as the lamination lay-up is commenced. Check for moisture, solvent, dust, finger marks, etc. on the gelcoat surface, prior to lamination lay-up.
	Gelcoat too fully cured (surface has lost its 'tackiness').	Check for wax additives in the gelcoat resin. Check catalyst levels. Avoid leaving the gelcoat on the mould for extended periods prior to laminate lay-up.
PROBLEM 10: Blistering of the gelcoat appearing shortly after 'pulling' or when moulding is in use.	Un-reacted catalyst.	Check catalyst quantities. Stir catalyst/resin mix thoroughly.
	Contamination, i.e. moisture, wax, acetone, etc.	Check mixing container and equipment carefully. Don't thin down resin with acetone.
	Dry laminate.	Check 'wet-out' technique. Ensure that laminating resin is thoroughly 'stippled' through the reinforcement material.

	Possible Cause	Action
PROBLEM 11: Sagging or 'curtaining' of the gelcoat on vertical areas of the mould before initial cure.	Excessive gelcoat thickness. Viscosity too low.	Improve application techniques. Check thixotropic property of the gelcoat being used. Shake or stir the drum prior to weighing out the gelcoat.
	Working temperature too low. Cold mould surface. Cold resin.	Do not attempt a gelcoat lay-up in cold conditions, i.e. under 12°C (53°F).
PROBLEM 12: Fading, bleaching or 'chalking', resulting in a loss of shine, or giving a streaky or chalk-like appearance to the gelcoat surface.	Incomplete cure of the gelcoat. Inadequate or unsuitable pigmentation.	Check catalyst quantities. Use adequate quantities of polyester pigments and dyes (not substitutes).
	Breakdown of gelcoat resin as a result of prolonged weathering.	Use good quality gelcoat resins and avoid thinning. Treat exposed GRP laminates with burnishing compounds and waxes.

Defects in the laminate

	Possible Cause	Action

PROBLEM 1: Laminate is 'resin starved'. Dry or porous areas are visible.

	Possible Cause	Action
(a) All over the laminate.	Poor or careless 'wet-out' technique.	Stipple or roll resin thoroughly through the laminate.
(b) In awkward areas.	Difficulty in applying glassfibre to the mould surface.	Pre-soak glassfibre on the bench before applying to mould.
(c) At the top edges of the moulding.	Poor or careless 'wet-out' technique.	As for (a). Always check top edges of the laminate on completion of the lay-up.
	Resin viscosity too high and so it cannot be stippled through the laminate *thoroughly*.	Often a result of using old resin which has suffered styrene evaporation. Up to 3% styrene can be added to the resin to reduce its viscosity.
	Working conditions too cold causing draining or 'puddling' of the resin. Exotherm too slow.	Check working temperature, draughts, cold resin, cold mould, etc. Check catalyst quantities. Check type of resin being used.

	Possible Cause	Action
PROBLEM 2: Laminate is 'resin rich'.	Poor or careless 'wet-out' technique.	Stipple or roll resin through the laminate more sparingly. Use a compression roller between layers.
	'Puddling' of the resin from vertical surfaces into the hollows of the mould.	Check viscosity of the resin, working temperature, catalyst, etc.
PROBLEM 3: Sagging of the laminate after 'pulling'.	Laminate too weak. Pulling from the mould while laminate is still green.	Increase lay-up thickness. Allow more cure time before pulling. Normally at least 24 hours.
PROBLEM 4: Warping of the laminate including 'print through' or distortion at reinforced areas.	Warping is caused by shrinking of the polyester resin in the laminate, during exotherm. Therefore the following conditions should be avoided as far as possible.	
	(a) High exotherm of the laminating resin.	Check catalyst levels.

	Possible Cause	Action
	(b) Lay-up too thick.	Maximum of 4 layers of 450 gm/m² (1½ oz/ft²) CSM or equivalent in other GRP materials. Allow time for exotherm heat to dissipate before continuing the lay-up.
	(c) Uneven thickness caused by over-laps, reinforcements, fittings laminated to shell, etc.	Allow sufficient time (24 hours minimum) between lay-up of shell and application of fittings, reinforcement materials, etc.
PROBLEM 5: Hot spots causing distortion or 'burning' of the laminating resin.	Over-catalysed resin. Resin rich areas. Uneven or too thick a lay-up.	Check catalyst/temperature chart. Work the resin through the glassfibre carefully. Work the resin through the glassfibre carefully.
PROBLEM 6: Soft spots.	Poor laminating technique. Unmixed catalyst. Contaminations of the laminate layers or the resin being used. Permanent under cure.	See 'resin starved' notes. Always stir in catalyst thoroughly. Ensure that no drops of water get on the glassfibre material. Evaporation of styrene from the resin. Keep resin drum sealed when not in use and use resin within the 'shelf life' period. Stir or shake the resin drum before decanting resin.

8 REPAIRS TO GRP LAMINATES

Glassfibre is one of the most straightforward structural materials on which to carry out repair work for a number of reasons.

1 The repair lay-up will readily adhere to the existing laminate surrounding the damage provided it is clean and dry. (An acetone wash and/or thorough sanding with coarse garnet paper will ensure a thorough bond.)
2 Damaged areas are usually fairly localised.
3 Frequently the damaged area will maintain its original shape because of the inherent resilience of the laminate. This makes repair work a great deal simpler.
4 By means of generous overlaps, carefully applied around the repair area, the original structural strength of the damaged laminate can be fully regained.

Gelcoat repairs
Most repair work is involved either with the gelcoat or the laminate, the gelcoat being the more vulnerable as it is usually the exterior surface.

Scratches
If shallow, these can be cut back with 600 grade 'wet and dry' paper and then polished out of the gelcoat using proprietary brand polishes or a metal polish such as Brasso. Deep scratches, should be cleaned with acetone, filled with matching gelcoat and then cut back and polished in the same way.

Chipping
All loose gel must be removed from the damaged area using a knife or chisel. Add pigment and catalyst to a small quantity of thixotropic resin and apply with spatula or putty knife. Cellophane adhesive tape can be used, if necessary, to hold the gel in place. After cure cut back and burnish the repaired areas as described for scratches.

Impact cracks
If the gelcoat surrounding the crack is still bonded firmly to the laminate, the crack is simply widened by scoring along it with a chisel, filling, cutting back and polishing as described for scratches. If, however, a number of cracks 'criss-cross', pieces of the gelcoat may have become delaminated from the glassfibre reinforcement and must be removed by prising them from the laminate with a knife or chisel. Masking tape should be placed around the damage and the same repair procedure followed as for chipping.

Scores
If deep scratches have penetrated the gelcoat and scored the laminate the external repair work is carried out as described for deep gelcoat scratches. However, the inside of the laminate may need to be backed up with layers of reinforcement, depending on the thickness of the moulding.

Shatter marks
If these impact marks appear white in colour on the inside of the moulding then the area has delaminated and must be completely removed. The edges of the hole are carefully chamfered, from both sides, to provide a good 'key' for the repair lay-up and a suitable covering (tinplate, Laminex, cellophane sheet, plywood, etc.) is taped to the gelcoat side of the work.

A suitably pigmented gelcoat is then applied to the covering working from the inside of the moulding. After cure, layers of CSM are carefully cut to the shape of the hole, pre-soaked and laid up on the gelcoat. When the thickness of the original shell has been built up, overlap layers are used to complete the bonding of the old laminate to the new. The covering is then removed and the new gelcoat area cut back and polished.

Unfortunately, it is almost impossible to achieve a perfect gelcoat colour match owing to fading and chalking of the original pigmentation during use. The best one can do is use some of the original gel for the repair, or quote the original pigment shade number when ordering touch-up gel. If, however, the cosmetics of the repair are important, as on the hull of a yacht, then the whole surface of the moulding may have to be sprayed with polyurethane paint.

Major laminate repair work

Major repair work is required when large areas of damage involving puncture of the GRP shell and possible detachment of pieces of the structure occur. Considerable difficulty can arise in attempting to achieve contour curves on the repair laminate which perfectly match the original shape of the damaged area. Depending on the complexity of the damage and the size of the moulding there are various methods of tackling the repair:

1 By taping, screwing or bolting some suitable material over the damaged area from the outside, and then rebuilding the damaged structure as for the repair of shatter marks. If, however, a large hole is to be covered this method is limited to flat surfaces or gently curving areas of the moulding.

2 By replacing the damaged moulding in its mould — after suitable mould preparation — and applying gelcoat and repair laminate against the mould in the usual manner. The specified thickness of the moulding is rebuilt and additional overlap layers of GRP ensure a strong, permanent repair. This method is, of course, limited by the size and weight of the moulding and the availability of the mould.

3 If the above method cannot be used a 'patch' mould can sometimes be fabricated against the outside of the damaged area. A repair patch is then laid up to the specified thickness of the moulding, and later laminated into position. This method involves temporarily piecing together the damaged parts of the moulding using tape, polyester filler, plaster, etc. After sanding smooth with garnet paper a polyester flow coat is applied, cut back and waxed to form the surface of the 'patch' mould.

This method takes time but reproduces perfectly, even the most complex curves in the moulding. Fitting of the patch is most accurately done by placing it over the damaged area of the laminate and, using a power jig saw, cutting through the periphery of the patch and the laminate of the moulding at the same time. The patch is heavily bonded to the moulding on the inside, the saw-cut filled from the outside and the whole gelcoat surface of the patch cut back and polished.

4 With this method the damaged area is cut out and the hole covered on the laminate side, using a sheet of marine-ply, which is potched and laminated against the moulding. A 'dough mix' or polyester filler is then used to build up and reshape the contours of the damaged area from the outside. After cure the filling is cut back and spray painted to match the surrounding gelcoat.

This method leaves a strong but clumsy patch on the inside of the moulding but if this does not matter (for instance where the patch is hidden behind internal fittings) then it provides a simple and effective means of repairing damage.

5 A method similar to the one above may sometimes be necessary in areas where there is no internal access to the damaged area. In this situation the splintered laminate is cut back and the edges bevelled in the usual manner, but the hole formed into an elliptical or rectangular shape — not a circle. A piece of marine-ply or aluminium sheet is then cut so that it slips through the hole at its widest part and can be held against the inside of the laminate by tensioning wires pulled from the outside.

This backing plate is first removed and a number of layers of CSM stippled onto it, then it is manoeuvred back into position and the wires tensioned to pull it outwards, squeezing the wet CSM against the edges of the hole. After cure the wires are cut off and additional layers of reinforcement laminate used to fill the gap and build up the original thickness. Alternatively, a dough mix or polyester filler can be used as described previously, to finish off the repair on the outside.

Maintenance of GRP mouldings

It is a common misconception that glassfibre mouldings are maintenance free. This is not so. With the passage of time the effects of weathering and the rigours of use take their toll of GRP as they do of all structural materials. However, if a little care and attention is paid to the gelcoat surface of a moulding, problems such as fading, chalking, crazing and porosity can be reduced. This, in turn, will help the gelcoat surface to resist abrasion and atmospheric dirt absorption and thus keep up the appearance of the moulding. A number of excellent burnishing compounds, which contain wax preparations, are available and should be applied at regular intervals.

Gelcoats should not be subjected to prolonged contact with petro-chemicals or staining and eventual penetration will result. The same applies to marine growth. A yacht moored in oily water or subject to weed and barnacles will suffer in this way, so an etch primer and anti-fouling paint must be applied beneath the waterline to give protection and prevent a build-up of growth. Trailered craft which are removed from the water after use do not need this protection, but should have their hulls scrubbed and waxed regularly to maintain appearance, performance and wear resistance.

The inside surface of a GRP moulding should also be treated with care and respect. Salt, sand and grit should be hosed out of boats and canoes so that abrasion of the laminate surface is kept to a minimum during use. Yacht and motor boat bilges should be kept clean by regular pumping and not left permanently in contact with oily water. A thorough application of flow coat will help to extend the working life of the laminate in most of these cases.

GLOSSARY

Accelerator A substance added to the catalysed resin which speeds up polymerisation reaction by the production of internal heat. Also called promoter or activator.

Acetone The most suitable cleaning solvent available for the removal of uncured resin from brushes, tools, clothing, etc. Acetone is a highly flammable liquid.

Additives Any substance added to the resin which imparts special performance properties, such as electrical conductivity, flame resistance and decorative effect.

A grade glassfibre A high alkali content glassfibre offering good resistance to attack by acids but rather poor resistance to moisture. A general purpose glass not suitable for marine or external use.

Air-inhibited resins These resins have their surface cures inhibited or stopped by the presence of air, thus allowing good chemical bonding between laminates.

Binder A bonding agent applied to chopped strand mat fibres to hold them in position in the mat structure. CSM can be resin or powder bonded.

Catalyst A peroxide, which, when added to the resin in small quantities causes rapid cure to take place. The catalyst oxidises the accelerator already contained in the resin, causing a heat build-up which starts the setting action.

Chopped strands The glassfibres, approximately 50 mm (2 in) long, cut from continuous filament roving, which are used to manufacture chopped strand mat. Chopped strands of glass can be blown directly onto the mould surface in spray-up techniques. They can also be milled up into 3 mm (⅛ in) lengths for use in GRP fillers. Fillers containing milled fibres are called 'dough mixes'.

Colour pigments Ground solids mixed in a suitable vehicle (usually a resin) to form a paste which can be easily mixed with gelcoat and laminating resins. Five to ten per cent pigment paste is added to give the required colour density.

Continuous filament An individual 'thread' of glass, of indefinite length, possessing enormous flexibility and strength. Bundles of filaments form strands which in turn can be twisted into rovings, woven into cloth or cut into short lengths for the production of CSM.

Core Any material which can be sandwiched between layers of GRP to give additional rigidity to the laminate.

CSM Chopped strand mat.

Cure The polymerisation process by which the resin is transformed from a liquid to a solid state.

Delamination Separation of the layers of glassfibre in a GRP laminate. Also used to describe the peeling or cracking of the gelcoat from the GRP reinforcement.

Density The weight of a substance per unit volume, i.e. lb/ft³ or gm/cm³.

Draw The release angle designed into a female mould which allows the moulding to be withdrawn from the mould without getting stuck in the process.

E grade glassfibre A low alkali content glass offering excellent resistance to water penetration. E grade glass is a high quality boro-silicate glass possessing good electrical insulation properties, hence the prefix 'E'.

Exothermic heat A chemically induced, internal heat build-up which causes the resin to commence its cure.

Fillers Any inert substance which is added to polyester resin to impart density or bulk to the work in hand.

Flow coat (brushing-out coat) A thin surface coat of polyester resin, usually coloured, which is applied to the rough inside surface of a moulding after cure. It forms a decorative and protective finish for the laminate.

Gel A partial cure of polyester resin. A semi-solid jelly-like state.

Gelcoat A surface coat of thixotropic polyester resin used to colour and protect the reinforcement layers of the moulding.

GP resin General purpose resin.

GRP Glassfibre reinforced plastics. The plastic is usually polyester resin and the reinforcement is usually in the form of CSM cloth, or woven rovings.

Hand lay-up The process of producing a GRP moulding, usually, inside a female mould, by means of brush and roller. The work is carried out at room temperature without the addition of external heat or pressure. Also called 'wet lay-up', 'low pressure moulding' and 'contact moulding'.

Heat-sink A substance which, when added to a large mix of polyester resin absorbs a proportion of the heat of polymerisation thus extending the initial cure time and reducing the exotherm. All fillers act as slight 'heat-sinks' as they all extend the pot life of the polyester mixture.

MEKP Methyl ethyl ketone peroxide.

Monomer The simple unpolymerised form of a compound as distinguished from a polymer.

Mould release coatings (parting agents) Substances used to treat the gelcoat surface of the mould to prevent adhesion of the lay-up.

Non-air-inhibited resin A resin in which the surface cure is not inhibited or stopped by the presence of air because a surfacing agent has been added to the resin.

NPG Neopentyl glycol.

'Open cup' flash point The lowest temperature at which a substance gives off sufficient vapours to form a flammable mixture with the air near its surface.

O.M. Outboard motor.

Polymers A group of chemicals which have a high molecular weight. Polymers can be changed from a liquid to a solid state by the cross-linking of their molecular structures.

Polyester resin A polymer whose chemical and mechanical properties make it ideally suited for use with glassfibre as a structural material.

Polymerisation The chemical reaction which takes place when the polyester resin commences its cure. The long molecular chains within the resin begin to cross-bond or link up, causing the substance to change from a liquid to a solid state.

Post cure Improved mechanical and chemical properties can sometimes be achieved by exposing the cured GRP laminate to higher temperatures than those prevailing in the workshop. This is normally done by passing the moulding through a 'kiln' or 'oven'.

Pot life The working life of polyester resin once it has been activated with catalyst and accelerator.

Potch A polyester filler made up by mixing the resin with equal ratios of either talcum powder or french chalk. It is a good general purpose filler and 'cement' for bonding GRP and plywood laminates.

PU foam Polyurethane foam.

Pull The expression used to describe the act of removing the moulding from its female mould.

PVA Polyvinyl alcohol solution.

SS Stainless steel.

Shelf life The length of time a pre-accelerated resin will remain workable while stored in a tightly sealed container.

Surfacing agent This is usually paraffin wax dissolved in styrene monomer. Called 'wax in styrene' or 'styrene wax'. Five per cent wax in styrene is added to flow coat resins. The wax rises to the surface of the resin during cure, and prevents the air from coming in contact with the polyester. This, in turn, allows the resin to achieve a total cure giving a non-tacky, glassy smooth finish. Small quantities of wax in styrene are also added to some grades of laminating resins and also some gelcoats.

Tack Stickiness experienced on the cured 'inside' surface of gelcoats and laminates. This tackiness allows good chemical bonding between gelcoat and reinforcement and also between successive layers of laminate in the lay-up.

Thermoplastics Materials which can be repeatedly softened and formed by heating, and hardened by cooling, e.g. acrylics, nylons and polyethylenes.

Thermosets Materials which undergo a chemical change when heated thus preventing them from reverting to their original state by further heating or chemical action.

Thinners Styrene monomer is the only thinner which should be used in polyester resin. It is also a 'co-reactant', i.e. it plays an integral part in the chemical change which takes place during polymerisation. Acetone should not be used as a thinner for polyester resin as it could cause various defects to appear in the moulding.

Thixotropic A term used in GRP work to describe the viscosity of the gelcoat and laminating resin. Thixotropic additives help prevent 'curtaining' of the gelcoat when it is applied to vertical surfaces. They also help reduce 'drainage' of laminating resin from the glassfibre during polymerisation. Aerosil powder is the thixotropic agent or filler most frequently used to increase the viscosity of polyester resin.

INDEX